MAKING THINGS RIGHT

MAKING THINGS RIGHT

THE SIMPLE PHILOSOPHY OF A WORKING LIFE

OLE THORSTENSEN

Translated from the Norwegian by Seán Kinsella

PENGUIN BOOKS

PENGUIN BOOKS

An imprint of Penguin Random House LLC
375 Hudson Street
New York, New York 10014
penguin.com

First published in Norwegian under the title
En Snekkes Dagbok by Pelikanen forlag 2015
First published in Great Britain by MacLehose Press,
an imprint of Quercus Publishing Ltd, 2017
Published in Penguin Books 2018

LIBRARY OF CONGRESS CATALOGING-IN-PUBLICATION DATA

Names: Thorstensen, Ole, author. | Kinsella, Seán (Translator) translator.
Title: Making things right : the simple philosophy of a working life / Ole
Thorstensen ; translated from the Norwegian by Seán Kinsella.
Other titles: En Snekkers Dagbok. English
Description: New York, New York : Penguin Books, an imprint of Penguin Random
House, LLC, 2018. | "Translated from the Norwegian. 1998."
Identifiers: LCCN 2017058279 (print) | LCCN 2017059361 (ebook) |
ISBN 9781524704780 (ebook) | ISBN 9780143130949
Subjects: LCSH: Dwellings—Remodeling—Norway—Anecdotes. |
Building—Technique. | Small business—Norway. | Thorstensen,
Ole—Philosophy. | Carpenters—Norway—Biography.
Classification: LCC TH4816 (ebook) | LCC TH4816 .T4813 2018 (print) |
DDC 690/.24—dc23
LC record available at https://lccn.loc.gov/2017058279

Printed in the United States of America
1   3   5   7   9   10   8   6   4   2

Set in Scala Regular

There are so many people to thank
but I do not want to forget anyone.

Torunn Borge has left us, she can
represent all of you.

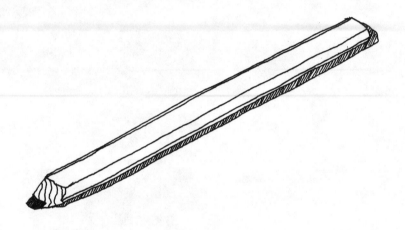

A glossary of terms is to be found on page 229

1

I WORK WITH WOOD. HAVING BEEN A CERTIFIED apprentice, I am now a qualified master craftsman, what most people refer to as a carpenter.

I learned the trade as an apprentice, and as a master I learned how to run a business. For me the craftsmanship, the work itself, is more meaningful than the management side; therefore my certificate of apprenticeship is more important to me.

There is nothing mysterious about skilled manual labor. My job is done to order and is wholly dependent upon demand, upon the instruction of others.

I am a contractor, an entrepreneur, and a businessman. These are the words used to describe what I do. I am a carpenter, this is the word I use, and I run a one-man carpentry firm.

The smaller firms in the building trade carry out what can be termed minor jobs, the larger companies are not that interested in those types of contracts. They are busy building whole new housing developments, hospitals, schools, sometimes a kindergarten and smaller commercial premises.

The smaller contractors put in new bathrooms, one by one; they replace windows in houses, and erect garages. They also build a lot of new houses, as well as the board and pole for the mailbox outside. A large amount of the maintenance and modernization of the almost two and a half million residences in Norway is carried out by smaller contractors.

There are a lot of us and we are to be found everywhere, so it goes without saying we are a diverse group. We are part of the same industry, we are tradesmen, and the fact that we approach our jobs in different ways is something tradesmen know better than anyone. We are fast, slow, good, bad, grumpy, happy, cheap, expensive, honest, and some of us are dishonest. All descriptions are relevant to the trade, with craftsmanship and its application.

I live in Tøyen in Oslo and work for the most part in the city, chiefly on the east side. Sometimes I work on the west side, and I have had jobs in places as far south of the city as Ski and Ås, and as far west as Asker. Not being native to Oslo, I have got to know the city through my job. When I am walking around the city with other people I can sometimes come to a halt, point, and say, I replaced a door in that place, I converted an attic in there, I renovated a bathroom in that house. For a man with no sense of direction it is a handy way to get to know the city, because I never forget a job I have done.

I have no employees, no office or premises of my own. My tools are kept in the storeroom of my flat, along with equipment and materials that cannot withstand frost, cannot be outside, such as glue and the like. Screws, nails, and all sorts of other things are up in the attic. My tools are an extension of me; by treating them with care I show the respect I have for the profession, the work, and for myself.

I park my vehicle, a slightly run-down panel van, wherever I find a spot for it in the streets around where I live. Every day after work I carry all my equipment up to my flat. Leaving tools lying in plain sight is not a good idea. Should anyone look through the windows they will see that the van is empty and there is no point in breaking in.

My flat is on the third floor, which entails lugging stuff up and down. I have become better at planning what is required for each job and now I take only what I need to when loading the van, saving time and avoiding too much back and forth.

My living room doubles as an office. The flat is not big, so I put any files and paperwork in a closed cabinet to keep them out of sight. Administrative work has to be done, but having the office at home like this can be tiresome. It feels as if I am always carrying a heavy rucksack, even after the trek is over. I never quite make it to a point where I can rest, take a break, and turn around to look back over the landscape I have passed through. When I have finished the work, the actual building, I have to open the cabinet, take out the relevant file, boot up the computer and pay VAT, write e-mails, archive documents, fill out forms, and calculate tenders. The hours I spend on this feel long, much longer than the hours I spend with materials and tools.

My company is a one-man business and there is no clear distinction between my private and professional life. I am in physical contact with the tools and materials I use and am likewise bound to the finances and consequences of my labor. There is a close connection between me and my drill, my van, the floor I am laying, the house I am building, and also the balance sheet.

At times this can feel overwhelming, but not simply in a negative way. It gives me a strong sense of my work not only being of great significance to the clients who ask me to reno-vate their homes but to me too. Financially and professionally,

I am exposed, devoid of the protection most people take for granted in their everyday working lives.

I make a living from producing transient objects that can be replaced and demolished. That is also a part of my profession. The things we surround ourselves with are crucial to our lives, and at the same time are unimportant, and that is the reason we can say that it went well, no lives were lost when the cathedral burned down.

The job I am currently doing in Kjelsås is nearing an end; in another three weeks I will be looking at blank pages in my appointment book. This is how it always is; I go to work and make something, while at the same time I keep an eye out for the next job.

2

I AM SITTING IN THE LIVING ROOM AT HOME. CAPTAIN
Beefheart is playing on the stereo, and outside it is a cold, wet
November evening. I was out late last night, so it feels fitting
when the Captain sings: "I went around all day with the moon
sticking in my eye." It is good music to wash up to so I make
a start on that, but I'm interrupted by the ringing of the
telephone. A number I do not recognize.

"Hello?"

"Hi. My name's Jon Petersen, I got your number from
Helene Karlsen."

"Ah, Helene and the boys, in Torshov. It's about some
building work, then?"

Helene and the boys were a family I did a loft conversion for
a couple of years ago. It was a nice job for a pleasant family.
Helene had a husband, and two sons, thus Helene and the
boys, as in the French sitcom popular in the 1990s. That was
what I called them, and they thought it was funny, I think, but
now it crosses my mind that of course Jon Petersen does not
know anything about that.

"Yes, we live in Torshov and have a loft we're also planning
to convert, so we're looking around for a contractor who

could do a good job. There are a lot of cowboys out there," he says, with an implicit tone to his voice.

"We want to use proper tradesmen, so when Helene told us how happy they were with the job you'd done and recommended you . . ."

Jon tells me a little about how Helene and the family have put their loft to use, and how they would like to do something similar with their own. The board of the housing cooperative for the building they live in have at long last agreed to part of the loft being converted into a living space. It can be difficult to get such things through in that system of home ownership— people can be wary of change and view it as unnecessary—but now they had finally bought the space and were ready to convert it.

"Can I ask you a few quick questions about the loft? Will the space be directly connected to the apartment you're already living in?"

"Yes, by way of a staircase up from the living room below. That's to say, we've already knocked through one wall, so it's open plan, with the living room and kitchen in one."

"Have you had drawings made and sought planning permission? Have you had a structural engineer's report carried out?"

We continue talking and Petersen tells me the plans are completed, and the engineer has provided specifications for the work and detailed drawings. They have applied for a building permit and expect it to be approved soon. I explain to him that should I get the job then I myself would carry out all the carpentry. The people I would subcontract to I have worked with for many years. It is an important distinction between contractors—there are those with their own people and those who outsource. There is a big difference between being a tradesman and being a recruitment agent or a wholesaler of tradesmen.

It turns out that the job is being put out to tender and I will be competing with two others. A good number; had it been five I would not have sent in a bid; the odds would have been too poor.

For Petersen, it would have meant picking out a contractor from a list where the best ones no longer featured, because I am not alone in my thinking, irrespective of whether I am among the best or not. A good contractor understands how to estimate these types of odds and this way of assessing the client. The clients who limit themselves to three quotations are increasing their chances of receiving a better quality of work than those who invite too many tenders and, in so doing, scare off the most competent tradesmen.

One way of doing it is to check out ten firms. The clients can examine their lists of references, their finances, and whatever else they might wish, before asking the firms they like the look of to spend time calculating a bid for the job. Supplying a list of references does not require much work, but preparing a quotation is time consuming.

If I am one of the three firms invited to compete for a job on those types of terms, then I am happy. I stand a reasonable chance of winning the bid.

The work I carried out for Helene and the boys now serves as a good reference; incidentally, they also invited tenders from a small number of firms.

During the course of our conversation, I learn that Jon works for Norwegian State Railways—in an administrative position, as he puts it. His wife, Kari, works for local government in the cultural sector. He hints that neither he nor she has much experience in converting a loft. He mentions this to indicate how little they themselves know about the practical side of a building project of this nature, to make it clear how dependent they will be on whoever gets the job.

The couple have two boys and need more space. They had started looking around for another place to live, but the opportunity of renovating came along and they took it. They like the apartment building they live in and the Torshov area, so they decided on a loft conversion.

Up to this point they have been dealing with the housing cooperative and the architect. Through him they have been in contact with the engineer and the planning office. The theoretical part of the process resembles what they encounter in their daily working lives and is therefore more understandable to them than what now needs to be done—the actual building. By now, Petersen has been working on the bureaucratic part of the process for more than a year. He is obviously impatient to move forward. It means I need to be careful not to add to his problems, add any more bricks to his load, or 2×4 boards in my case.

The advantage of paperwork is that it is reversible; it means little as long as it is not put into practice, but I cannot relate to what has been put down on paper as anything other than a kind of reality. I cannot build something just to see if it works, tear it down, and build anew. I could, if the customer would pay for it, but that is highly unlikely.

For me, theory is something I translate into images of the completed work. I count screws, nails, yards of materials, and I calculate hours. I create a film in my mind of how I want the building work to proceed, and the drawings and specifications are the script. The clients are most interested in the result, in what they see when the tradesman tells them he is finished, but in a way they are better able to understand the description on paper.

When the job is done the plans and specs are forgotten about, are not important anymore. They are the connection between the loft as it is and what it will be.

I am occupied with what is to be done, while to a large extent, the client, the architect, and the engineer take that for granted. This divergence of focus often creates a distance between the architect and the engineer on one side, and me as the craftsman on the other.

I think most tradesmen are in the same position—we miss the architect on site, would like him or her to be available to enter into a direct dialogue with us to find solutions that are in the client's best interest.

In most cases the architect scarcely visits the site, and often the engineers do not set foot there prior to making their calculations. I sometimes manage to coax them out of their offices; at least that is what it feels as though I am doing. On the occasions I do, the solutions we arrive at to problems that have cropped up are generally better than they would have been otherwise. Better in a financial sense, in terms of the quality of the build, and in the case of a loft conversion, they make it a better place to live.

The level of cooperation between the academic side of the construction industry and the artisanal has deteriorated in the course of my twenty-five years in the business. The building trade has become more academic. At the same time, the custom of tradesmen actively using their expertise to influence the building process has declined. Previously, it was a natural part of professional practice. But considered thought and reflection dwindle when a variety of informed opinions are not heard.

When you are not taught a more collaborative way of working, then you do not know what you are missing. I think many architects and engineers wish the culture were different; they would like cooperation placed to the fore, and I believe that the present situation is self-reinforcing. This applies to all parties in the business; we are so accustomed to this factional manner of working that we take it for granted.

These ground rules are not drawn up according to an industry standard, which means that each tradesman has to be smart in his dealings with all the others, with the clients, architects, and the engineers. The expression "two sides of the same coin" is very apt in this regard.

3

I LIKE WORKING ON LOFT CONVERSIONS.

I like the atmosphere, support structures, fire safety aspects, finish, materials, and customer contact. I like how the choices you make are both immediate and long term. It is work with visible results, where you start off with something old, history wherever you lay your hand, and end up with something completely different and new.

On these kinds of jobs I picture myself as taking over and completing work someone else carried out 130 years ago. As though the building phases occur after long intervals yet form part of a coherent process. A drying loft was important in the past, but no longer serves any function and is now more likely to be used as a storage space. We do have a lot of stuff to store nowadays. I can find traces of 130 years of activity in a loft like that, and while working I am at close quarters to this history. Water damage, clotheslines, old wiring, air ducts, and perhaps asbestos.

The apartment building where Petersen lives, on Hegermanns gate, was erected around 1890. Electrical installation was becoming commonplace in these buildings from around the turn of the last century. On occasion I will come across remnants of the first electrical systems, disconnected, but not dismantled: black wiring, passing through porcelain knob tubes supported by porcelain knob insulators. Any asbestos around ventilation ducts probably dates from around 1930.

The newspapers that turn up in the walls and lofts of old buildings tell you something about the people who lived there. In 1930, your choice of newspaper was more closely linked to your political outlook. *Aftenposten* and *Norges Handels og Sjøfartstidende*, the conservative trade journal. It is unlikely that a Labor Party voter owned that storeroom. While a copy of *Nationen* probably belonged to a city dweller originally from the provinces. *Arbeiderbladet* is the newspaper I most commonly come across on the east side of the city.

I have a copy of *Fritt Folk*, the newspaper of Quisling's party, dated May 1945, lying somewhere at home. It describes German defensive victories. I found it in a loft in Vogts gate, and have sometimes wondered why the occupant held on to it. Was it for the same reason as I have, as a historic curiosity, or had it more to do with their political sympathies?

The roof construction of old lofts is impressive, elegant, and precise. All the parts have a clear function. They are built on logic, with beautiful, rough, detailed craftsmanship. The building technique they used, with heavy timber framework, is typical of the carpentry to be found in the rest of these apartment buildings. Writing and roman numerals are etched into the frame, like numbers on a life-size model kit. It is an early form of prefabrication which shows that whoever built this was not wasting time, a significant and unchanging feature of good workmanship.

They made drawings of the construction, manufactured the individual parts somewhere they could work effectively, and then assembled them swiftly on site. A working process intended to leave as little as possible to chance. It is a simple construction but requires a demanding method of building from a craftsman's perspective, one that few carpenters master these days. I build in a contemporary way, with the knowledge I have, for the needs of our day and age.

4

JON PETERSEN SENDS ME THE ARCHITECT'S PLANS AND
the engineer's drawings, along with the specifications, a simple
description of the work. Using these as a basis I will price a
job at more than $125,000. When the loft is finished and
the Petersen family move in, it will look as it does in the drawing, only fifty times larger. It is like the model airplanes
I used to build when I was a little boy, only in this case it is
the contents—or occupants—of the model that matter. And,
unlike in a kit, the parts are neither complete nor numbered.

I look at the plans, knowing they will take a little time
to sink in, and that I will need to visit the loft and speak to
the client to perfectly understand what they have in mind, what
it is precisely that they want. There is a reason for every
architect's plan. Some are a result of the building as it stands.
Others derive from the client's conception of what they want.
I use the word *conception*. The plans may show something
far removed from what the client originally wanted, and what
is finally built might be even further removed. I can sympathize; personally I too need time to grasp drawings and the
ideas behind them. It is easier for me to build when I am aware
of and understand the reasons for the loft to be constructed
as described.

According to the plans, the part of the loft to be converted covers a floor space of almost 650 square feet. This area is to contain a bedroom, a living room, and a bathroom. The existing stairwell will be built into the room with a mezzanine, or galleried floor, under the roof. The door to the stairwell will be the escape route in the event of a fire. The attic will be connected to the apartment beneath by a new half-turn staircase. The flooring will be solid wood, not parquet. Spending a little more money on that is smart; it lasts longer and looks a lot better in my opinion. It is nice to get the opportunity to lay a solid wood floor once in a while.

I try to take in the drawings, as if the whole thing has been built as described, as though I am standing in the loft eight months and a good $125,000 from now. It has to be allowed to sink in. That requires time. But as long as I am aware of having to work that little bit extra to understand the specifications, it is not wasted time.

Sometimes I have to tease things out of the client, aggravate them almost, pose questions: Why is such and such to be where it is; yes I can see that, but why exactly? Make them explain, put what they are thinking into words. Then I let the questions ferment, and after about a week I pose them anew and get a better answer. I do it just as much for my own sake, to get my own head around it, as for the customer to understand how it will turn out if we do it this way or that. We need to understand it in the same way.

The fact that the customer knows they are the one footing the bill should not be underestimated. Neither should her personality, nor my own.

Some clients have a need to be in control. In which case I have to be shrewd in order to get my opinions and points of

MEZZANINE

DOOR —TO EXISTING STAIRWELL

KIDS' ROOM

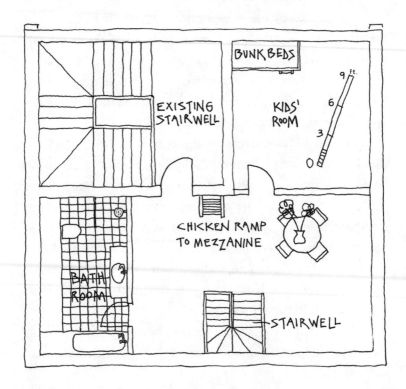

BUNK BEDS

EXISTING STAIRWELL

KIDS' ROOM

9 ft.

6

3

0

CHICKEN RAMP TO MEZZANINE

BATH ROOM

STAIRWELL

view across. Other clients gladly leave most of the decisions to others.

Do what you think is best, they say. They place a lot of trust in you, but they can at the same time be the most difficult customers since they often have trouble making decisions. So I need to make them understand that I am building for them, and they need to make the choices themselves. If we misunderstand one another they all end up equally dissatisfied, no matter what type of customers they are, and it is up to me to avoid that.

Money is important; costs must not exceed what the customer is able, or willing, to pay. Pricewise, doing something one way or the other is often much of a muchness. From the client's perspective, it is a matter of making the right choice.

Nevertheless, almost everybody who has building work carried out does so with half a mind on what an estate agent will say. Even though they may intend living there for years to come, they will build with a view to what is best with regard to buying and selling. Because this is combined with an excessive consumption of interior design magazines, it results in so many dwellings looking similar. The current fashion for various shades of white, gray, and light bluish gray on the outer walls of houses is one example. Due to unwritten laws and norms, bathrooms nowadays look for the most part like variations of tiled rooms in an abattoir. Kitchens seem to have all been designed by the same consultants at Ikea, or their counterparts at similar manufacturers like Norema. And when I say a consultant, I do not mean a specialist in their field, like an architect with a sense for interior design or a good craftsman. A consultant, in this case, is a salesperson in a shop.

The specifications and scope of the job in hand are so

imprecise that I have a few questions for the architect. I would like to know if he is intending to make more detailed plans. I am also wondering about the description of the load-bearing structures of the building's roof. There is no mention of what is to be done with the brick walls. Nor are the tiles in the bathroom described.

The architect, Christian Herlovsen, is dismissive when I call him. I am to make do with the documents at my disposal.

5

IT IS THURSDAY EVENING AND I AM IN TORSHOV, standing outside the apartment building in Hegermanns gate. I view the property from across the street. The gray painted facade is simple, free of adornment and artifice. I like it, though. Many people like stucco on exterior walls and cake decoration around the windows, but I think simple facades are lovely. The building would previously have had the same stately look as all the other buildings from around 1890. They bought in ornamentation by the yard and mounted it pretty much as I install skirting and trim. The current facade is probably the result of a renovation in the 1950s. It is as much a part of the building's history as what went before.

The pavement is wide and parking is allowed on the street. That means I will have space for a crane truck and containers, or skips. The entrances to the building face right onto the pavement, as opposed to a covered entranceway providing access to the rear and a way up to the apartments from there, as is often the case. The entranceway leads into a courtyard but it is not intended for vehicular access. However, it could prove useful if temporary storage on street level is required.

The walk up the stairs provides a preliminary survey of the site. There is information to be found everywhere. The space

available in the stairwell is important as regards the ease or difficulty with which you can transport materials. Is there enough room to be able easily to carry boards; is it possible to send longer materials up between the banisters in the center of the stairwell? Has it been painted recently? If so, you have to be particularly mindful of the walls.

The specifications make no mention about fireproofing in the entrance area and the staircase. Converting the loft will mean additional measures to comply with fire-safety regulations for this entire stairwell. The door down to the basement and the apartment doors have been replaced and look as if they adhere to the regulations. The necessary drywall, or plasterboard, work has also been carried out from the basement up. That leaves little doubt that fire protection has been taken into account and that the absence of any reference to fireproofing in these areas is not due to an oversight in the specifications.

Jon says hello and introduces me to Kari. The children are at their grandparents' this evening. Our first meeting, and perhaps our last. They want to see me, assess me. They seem pleasant; I am sizing them up as much as they are me. We sit at the kitchen table for a while, studying the plans. We talk about the project in general, while I slip in a few questions about details to show that I understand the job, as well as to give the impression I am interested, which I am. It is of course important to find out as much as possible about the project, but it takes time to get an overview and right now it is initial impressions that count. This is the first round and it needs to go well if I am to get the job. How you relate to one another even across a table says a lot about how you will be able cooperate when things become serious. It is important to find out if you can get along.

Having spoken to Jon a couple of times, and now meeting Kari, the two of them become "the Petersens" in my head. We go up to the loft, where it is pretty dark. I put on my LED headlamp to see better into the nooks and crannies and place my Mac on a stool. I write down the information they give me, their answers to the questions I ask, as well as taking note of any issues I need to remember for later.

Winter is an impractical time of the year for many types of site inspections, with the darkness and snow covering features you would prefer were in plain view. All the same, it is nice with the muffled acoustics and the stars shining so early in the evening. Even in the city you can make some out.

I stick my head out of the old skylight and take a look around, at the chimneys, vent guards and as much of the roof as I can see. The darkness makes me feel I am in a scene from *The Hunchback of Notre Dame*. A crescent moon appears between two chimney stacks standing close together, looking like a cutting tool that has divided a larger chimney and placed the two parts back down again a little distance from one another. The snow makes it impossible to see the condition of the flashings or how they look where they meet the slates.

The roof was replaced eight years ago and should be OK; the chimneys were also checked out and ought to be in good condition. Constructionwise, the loft is similar to other top-story spaces in Oslo from around the end of the nineteenth century. It is large and spacious, 15 to 20 feet to the ridge of the roof, with collar beams, ties, and struts—all the things so many people think look nice, which take up a lot of space and get in the way. The urban variant of rustic romanticism. The roof pitch is quite steep, and the knee walls are high, making it a good loft to convert since it will be roomy under the ceiling.

The shaft of the stairwell stands like a cube in the loft and will remain after the renovation, a mezzanine on top. The firewall that needs to be constructed will end around that cube.

The storage rooms are simple, airy spaces constructed from wood and dating from when the whole building was new. Some of them will be moved from what is to become the living space into what will remain of the drying loft. Although little of that area is to be retained, there will be sufficient space for storage rooms.

The electricity, telephone, and television cables are in a tangle and will all need to be rewired or relocated. A lot of it can be removed. The television and telephone people need to be contacted at an early stage; generally they are hard to get hold of and take their time coming round. Cutting off people's connections to the outside world is not something to be treated lightly. You do not want to annoy neighbors with such an inconvenience when you already represent noise and dust. You can quickly fall to the level of a wood-boring beetle or some other unwanted pest in their eyes. There may already have been numerous alterations and renovations carried out in the building prior to the arrival of another tradesman coming to convert the loft, and further work can be perceived as part of an interminable period of racket and mess. Understandably, people can get fed up with the property they live in being a building site.

I have made notes on matters that I have not yet mentioned to the Petersens. It is too early to talk about them, even though it would be good to bring them to their attention: two ventilation ducts insulated with asbestos need taking care of. The ventilation needs to be rebuilt with new pipes, which will have to be led up through the roof, and then new caps installed.

A soil pipe, or waste pipe, needs to be removed, or relocated, to be more precise. Two soot lids need shifting out. A brick ventilation shaft has been partially demolished just below the roof, but it has not been sealed on top. I have no idea what was going through the mind of whoever did this, but essentially they have created a firetrap. A fire could spread via this brick shaft to the loft and the smoke would have a clear path up. The shaft needs to be led up through the roof by way of insulated ventilation pipes. This is a serious error.

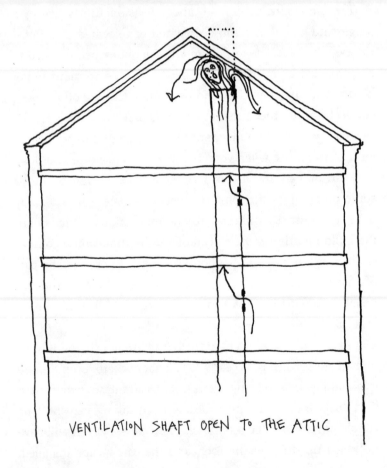

VENTILATION SHAFT OPEN TO THE ATTIC

The Petersens have mentioned their desire for quality while avoiding unforeseen expense, about wanting to know what things are going to cost as early as possible. The list of things I have noticed so far is not long and the extra work to be done will not cost much in relation to the total cost of the project. Nevertheless, the outlay will be considerable. These are points the architect has not included in his specifications. Why has he left them out? Maybe because pointing out extra expenses is not popular, as though the expenses are connected to you, and so it is better to look the other way and leave the job to someone else. This has become a culture, a way of working. See no evil, hear no evil. When it is impossible not to see or hear then all you are left with is the last possibility, speak no evil.

Issues and difficulties, which are really just a normal part of the building process, become in this way problems that are set aside until they prove impossible to ignore. Generally, this happens when the physical work gets under way and they land in the lap of the tradesman, who then is required to inform the customer. It is easy, then, to associate the tradesman with someone who sees problems.

I prefer to be up-front and honest and make them aware of everything I see, the good and the bad. I would like them to find out about these types of things early on, but I cannot tell them now, because that would reduce my chances of landing the job. It will have to wait until later.

I also need to curb the enthusiasm I feel with regard to the job. All the same, I have a film rolling in my head where larger aspects and smaller details are being picked up on and I see the whole thing taking shape. I picture the rafters and ceiling beams fitting where they ought to go, the new with the old, before being covered up behind drywall, not to be seen again by anyone for another fifty or a hundred years. A person like me perhaps, with a film rolling in their head all day long. This futuristic colleague of mine is different from me, yet similar in many ways. He or she might, without ever having known me, spare me a kind thought due to the quality of the work that becomes visible as things are torn down. What I have done has been done with care, and that will be apparent to those who are able and willing to see it, sometime in the future. That is at any rate how I am now viewing the loft and how I think of those who built it. I could have told the Petersens that it will mean a lot should the family be willing to put their faith in me, to allow me to convert their loft for them, but that is not how things work. I have to wait my turn, behind the architect, the structural engineer, and the caseworker at the planning department, all of whom outrank me in some indefinable way.

I can speak for myself, but in a cautious, modest manner, bordering on subservient, because that is the order of things in a practical, psychological, and social sense. The architect has perhaps twenty or thirty jobs like this in the time it takes me to build what he has drawn. The structural engineer may manage to carry out the necessary calculations for a hundred lofts in the time it takes me to renovate one.

I think I put more of my heart and soul into a job like this than they do. That opinion is not based purely on time spent, but also on the levels of dedication I have witnessed from architects and engineers I have worked with on jobs like this.

For me, this job is almost half a year's revenue and I am going to get sweaty and dirty, bang my thumb, cut myself, as well as freeze while I am doing it. This job, should I get it, will define me during a specific period in my life.

I would like to be judged on the basis of my profession, as though the profession itself is a person. So my notion of the competent craftsman appraising the quality of my work at some future date is very personal. I think a lot of the men who were builders more than a hundred years ago thought the same way. We form a long line of coworkers, friends almost, in my head.

6

THE JOB I AM BUSY WITH ON SIRIUSVEIEN IN KJELSÅS
is well on schedule. I am replacing a few windows, putting
down decking, and doing a number of other odds and ends.
The house owners are not using the outside area at this time
of year and they are nice clients, so I get the green light from
them to postpone the remaining work for a couple of days to
allow me time to calculate a quote for the Petersens.

The site survey went well; I managed to take everything in
properly, adjust my perspective so the drawings related better
to what I saw in front of me. Sometimes when taking a look at
a place I will immediately know that a second visit is inevitable
so as to take absolutely everything in. Having an overview and
confidence is crucial when working out an offer for a job of
this size. The total cost will run to over $125,000, with six or
seven hundred man-hours needed in carpentry alone. If I err
and price the job too low it will prove expensive for me. Should
my price be too high I will not get the job.

The architect has prepared an itemized description of the
work with estimates of material quantities for the main parts
of the project. This description lacks detail, as the following
serves to illustrate: "walls and ceiling plastered, primed and
given two coats of paint, solid pine flooring treated with lye

and oiled. Two Velux skylights 30 × 62 in and two Velux skylights 21 × 30 in; windows lined with drywall bathroom interior decor Ikea," and so on. All in all, the drawings and specifications are vague and quite risky to follow.

I could mention my list of additional work needed and make it clear that it is not included in the bid since it was not mentioned in their itemization. I could also decline to mention it, but it would feel underhand not to draw their attention to it.

In any case, I have to specify what I am quoting a price for, but I must not be too detailed. If I spend too much time on it I am at risk of offering a free consultation. I have experienced, many times previously, my bid and descriptions being passed on to another firm, who go on to carry out the work.

On a project like this, the contractors spend a considerable amount of time before a single nail is hammered in. A rough estimate can help make this clearer.

Suppose four contractors use four days each, sixteen working days in total, calculating a quotation. The four main contractors request price estimates from their subcontractors, of which there are five, for each part of the job: masonry; electrical systems; heating, ventilating, and air-conditioning (HVAC); plumbing; and painting and decorating.

Multiply four main contractors by the five quotations from the subcontractors and the total is twenty. If my subcontractors use one day on each bid, including a visit to the site, then that makes for twenty days. Total working days for all four main contractors comes to sixteen, and twenty for the subcontractors. So, all in all, thirty-six working days on a tender like this one, if the drawings and specifications are good.

Thirty-six days at eight hours a day is 288 hours, and if you multiply that by a $65 hourly rate, then this bidding round costs $18,720 before VAT.

When there are four firms vying for the job, you have a 25 percent chance of winning the bid, and on average you would normally have to put in the work for four tenders of this type in order to get one.

Then the cost of getting a job of this kind is $18,720, or 288 man-hours. That is a lot of work to get a job.

The tender drawings and specifications are fundamental because they set forth what is to be done. In the beginning was the word, as they say. The architect and the engineer are the ones who produce these documents, which I use to base my estimate on. Often it can appear as though the job they do is seen as more important and more difficult than that of the tradesman. If the tradesman feels the description is lacking then it is hard for him to offer a correct quotation and thus avoid conflicts and disagreements with the clients.

Sometimes it almost seems as though the architects retreat when a difficulty arises, that they imagine the client and the tradesman will sort it out between them. The conceptual design is perhaps more reasonable for the customer, and it looks good on paper, but it can prove expensive when a job is to be carried out without a satisfactory description, with extra costs being incurred that the client has not budgeted for, or simply with flaws and defects in the work.

Professional experience of the practical side, of being in touch with tradesmen, such as would offer them more insight into the actual craftwork, is steadily declining among architects and engineers.

Irrespective of whether this is the aim of an architect or engineer, the consequences are considerable. I believe it to be a major deficiency in their professions, but they get away with it because their work has greater prestige than that of a tradesman. This is a claim that is, of course, hard to substantiate, but I think many of those involved in the practical side of building work will recognize what I am talking about.

That the idea or conception of something is adjudged superior to its concrete implementation is a natural consequence of a society in which theory has become increasingly important. The execution is dirty and imprecise, while the idea is pure and unsullied. Theory is always flawless, until you try to apply it in practice and get human fallibilities and material faults thrown into the mix. There is a limited possibility of drawings being wrong; they are after all only lines on paper—hygienic, minimalistic, and blameless. Craftsmanship is almost the opposite.

It is actually rather odd that this type of thing should be knocking about my head each time I work on a tender. I would sooner just think about the job, but I have to be a psychologist, sociologist, anthropologist, and historian, in addition to being what I ought to be: a tradesman with a vague understanding of microeconomics and of the law.

The sketchy tender documentation can also result in the customer comparing apples and oranges, as the different contractors do not think the same way, nor do they interpret the description of the job in the same manner. If one of my competitors has not gleaned as much as I have in their reading of the supporting attachments, but he still wins the bid, I have lost out anyway. Being right does not pay any bills, so it is of little or no consolation should the job end up with a load of extra expenses and possible conflict between the client and my competitor.

The skilled contractors are measured against firms which offer cut-price rates for jobs because that is the only way they can get the work. The financial side, the price, is in many respects the final basis for comparison, outweighing matters of professional competence and quality of work. This under-pricing has considerable consequences for how the building market operates.

Contractors swap many stories in the course of a working year, ones in which new bathrooms have to be torn out, general demolish-and-rebuild stories. It is not rare for a contractor to be asked to come and look at a job once more, only this time it is finished and the work has been carried out by a competitor. The contractor is then asked if he can redo the job, fix things up. Rectifying other people's work is no fun, but when it is so bad that it involves entirely renovating a bathroom, it is just sad. Being a carpenter, my favorite stories are generally those about load-bearing structures that are ruined due to someone having removed important parts, leaving everything to rest mostly on goodwill.

Fixing your own mistakes is a given. Preferably they will be small ones, but leaving behind work you cannot vouch for is simply besmearing your reputation. When I was serving my apprenticeship, my old boss always told me to relax when I had done something stupid. He was stricter when the job was going all right than when something went awry. In time I understood the point was that I should take responsibility for the poor work I had done, as much as I should expect praise for what I had done well. As long as I knew it was just a matter of putting something right, then asking for help was no big deal. There is shame bound up with having to admit an error. But finding mistakes and correcting them is a natural part of the job and it leads to a better result. I do not always manage to be so patient with others myself, and can get worked up when something happens that I do not like. At times like that I need to calm down and apologize afterward. My old boss exemplifies to me now how things should be done. I remember the expressions he used and have made them my own. The fact that I do not always follow my own rules does not make them wrong.

As my old boss used to say, I have no problem eating humble pie, so long as I am the one who bakes it. So I offer an apology for my behavior when I realize it is called for, and I fix the mistakes I make when I have to. Well, on the occasions when I can see them, that is.

7

THERE IS A BIG HOLE IN THE PROJECT BRIEF. I DID NOT
spot it on the first reading or on visiting the site, but I see it
now. The plan drawings show a nice bathroom with a bench
running along one long wall and a sink cabinet on the wall
opposite. The shower and toilet are to be at one end of the room
and the bathtub at the other.

It would have been a lovely bathroom if the architect
had taken the struts and ties reinforcing the roof rafters into
account. The loft is like all others of this type and these components are there for a reason. They help hold the roof up, but
they will have to be removed if there is to be room for the
bathtub.

When alterations like this are carried out the roof has to be
reinforced. With insulation now being planned for the loft,
less heat will escape through the roof, meaning that the snow
will take longer to melt and it will have to bear more weight
for longer. The roof has to meet contemporary load standards
when it is rebuilt and these are stricter than in the past.

The engineer has taken this into account and the calculations for reinforcing the roof are attached, but they are
dependent on the struts and ties remaining in place. In which
case the Petersens or their children will almost certainly

complain about having to lie under one of the ties when taking a bath. Inconvenient no doubt, but nowhere near as impractical as having to sit perched on the tie at the other end when they want to go to the toilet.

Neither the architect nor engineer has thought of this. New solutions are needed for the support construction, and the engineer is going to have to carry out his job one more time.

Support constructions are simple in principle: everything must rest on the ground—Newton's apple, the first lesson in gravity. The construction of the loft is not as complicated as the new bridge over Hardanger fjord but the solution is not obvious at first blush. The problem now is to find a reasonable solution in terms of cost, in terms of also looking good, and which can be easily built.

First, I need to find the solution, then explain what the problem is. Doing it in that order may mean I make a good impression on the Petersens and that could help when it comes to them choosing a contractor.

I chew on the problem and come up with an answer so simple that I will be happy to see it work, whether I get the job or not.

I make a sketch and call Jon Petersen to explain the problem. After Petersen has felt dejected for a day, and has had time to share his despondency with the architect, I get in touch again. I tell him I have an idea, but I will need a little more time to knock up a sketch, even though that is already done. I want them to realize that this requires extra effort on my part. I ask him if he would like me to do this. I then ask him if he would like me to have a chat with the architect and the engineer. If so, could he give them a ring beforehand, so they are aware I am going to call? Absolutely, yes, yes, thank you.

Then comes the million-dollar question:

"Ehm . . . what will this cost?"

"Nothing," I say. "Consider it service, and I want the job, so I'm hoping this stands me in good stead."

I tell him that and mean what I say, but it still feels like I am selling myself cheap while I crawl with head held high. I have learned my lesson—you need to sell yourself as though you are a commodity. I used not to be so tactically minded, or cunning, as you could call it. It does not make me feel good, but after you have been fooled and taken advantage of a few times you understand. I am a craft product.

Petersen has called the architect and now it is my turn. Christian Herlovsen is part owner of a small firm. I had not heard of him prior to the tender round for this job, but I have checked him out on the Internet. He has been involved in several projects of a similar size, so he should know what he is doing. He understands the problem and is interested in finding a solution. I let the conversation run on so that eventually he asks me if I have any suggestions, and I tell him I do.

Though he had been offhand when we first spoke, the architect is not so dismissive now, but it is difficult for him to acknowledge that I am right, perhaps even to commend me for having noticed a problem, and even for having taken the time to find a solution.

I explain my idea and it meets with his approval, leaving me to now call the engineer and consult free of charge for a little longer. I text Petersen to be sure that he has got in touch with the engineer to let him know I will ring him, as well as to show Petersen I am busy on his behalf.

This is fun, although it would be a lot more so if we dropped the game and really worked together, preferably on a job I got paid for. All the same it only takes me a few hours in total. The experience is akin to being a schoolboy and a teacher at the same time, as well as reaffirming to me the eternal truth about supply and demand in business, albeit seen from a low rung on the ladder of the building trade.

Halvorsen, the structural engineer, seems surprised at my call, even though he has been forewarned by Petersen, and he is busy, as engineers often are. We arrange to talk on the telephone the following day.

So, Friday morning and the telephone conversation with the engineer. It was not possible for him to meet me on-site, where to my mind it would have been easier to envisage the solution. As I suspected, he has only seen the architect's drawings and he does not deem it necessary to actually inspect the site now either; the plans have been dimensioned, after all.

I outline the problem and what needs to be done. The ties and struts running along the walls need to go; he agrees with me on that. So, I explain the solution:

"We redo the construction to make it a roof truss with a ridge beam. At the gable wall we place the beam in a cavity and brick around it. At the opposite end we place the beam on a post resting on the wall of the stairwell.

"That should work, right?"

After a pause for thought, Halvorsen agrees.

"The only thing is that the rafters will be weakened when we remove those ties and struts, and would need to be reinforced," he says.

"Yes," I say. "We can reinforce them with 2×9s which we glue and nail, as many as necessary. And then put in new rafters between the old ones, so that we double the number of rafters in the roof. We use 2×9s for them as well."

He wants to use Kerto beams. I tell him that 2×9s will do fine, but he will need to work out how many will be required. They will have to be of C30 quality instead of the usual C24, as they will be that much stiffer. The same goes for the work to be done on the floor. That grade of wood is reasonably priced and good to work with.

"Yes, of course," he says.

Step by step we agree on the process.

"To give the new rafters something to rest upon at the knee wall we run a 2×9 beneath them. We fix that to the wall so that it can bear the load."

He agrees, but thinks we might need two planks. He will do some sums on it.

"The ties and struts can then be removed, right?"

They can, which makes us both happy, but I am not quite finished.

"The client could get a much better layout to the mezzanine over the stairwell if we moved the beam to the side of the ridge. Then neither the beam, nor the post it is to rest on at that end, will be in the way of the steps up to the area above. There is a good height up in that galleried area, beneath the middle of the roof, so it would be a shame to lose any head-room because of that large beam. The chicken ramp has to be placed right beneath the ridge anyway since it cannot be in the way of the door out to the stairwell, and that door is not directly under the ridge."

"Of course!" Now he comes to life again.

Soon that solution is in the box as well. He explains approximately how far to the side of the ridge of the roof the beam can go, taking his time to explain how the forces in the roof construction work if we move the beam in that way, about

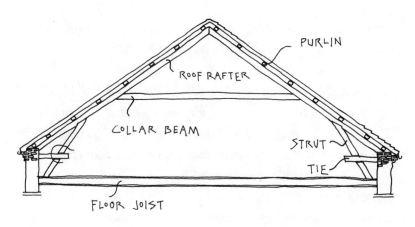

PURLIN

ROOF RAFTER

COLLAR BEAM

STRUT

TIE

FLOOR JOIST

ORIGINAL CONSTRUCTION

0   3   6   9   12 ft.

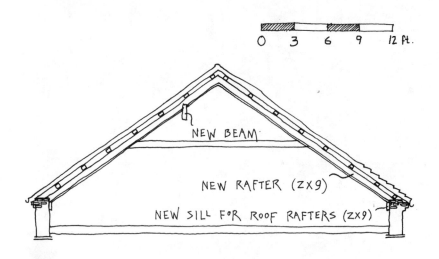

NEW BEAM

NEW RAFTER (2X9)

NEW SILL FOR ROOF RAFTERS (2X9)

NEW CONSTRUCTION

39

where the tipping point occurs and where the loads become greater.

"On top of everything else, I've learned something new today," I say.

Halvorsen is OK. He seems to be enjoying our chat now and even has time to spare. We talk a little more about building, and about life in general, before saying our goodbyes.

He will now make a drawing and send it to Herlovsen the architect, who will incorporate it into the project plan.

It is Friday; it has been a good day and I want to take the evening off. I can look at the figures and work out a bid tomorrow. Tomorrow, tomorrow, just another day.

8

I TAKE A STEAMING HOT SHOWER, USING PLENTY OF SOAP
and a nailbrush. The job in Kjelsås has been dusty and dirty
over the last few days. There has been a lot of demolition work.
The dirt is still lodged in the pores and cracks of my skin; it
is impossible to remove altogether. My hands are scrubbed
and as clean as can be and that is the most important thing.

I like my hands; they have been formed by my age and my
work. Some scars, none of them large, all the fingers intact,
they are my work: carpenter's hands. The skin is hard, yet free
of calluses; it is a long time since I have had them. The skin
on them is like a thin work glove. My history can be read in
them, I think; my hands look like what I have done and do
in life. They are a testimonial, my personal CV.

Sheet metal workers and bricklayers have strong paws. The
former work a lot with pliers and often cut themselves on sharp
metal edges. It shows. Masons lift blocks, heavy buckets, and
sacks. Cement, mortar, and grout are not exactly moisturizers
for the skin, perhaps more of an extra-abrasive exfoliant.
Compared to the people in those lines of work I have nice,
delicate hands.

I feel at home in Teddy's Bar; it is like my second living
room. I get there early, in the afternoon, time for a beer and a

burger. Johan, Espen, and Christer are sitting at the corner of the bar. You do not need to arrange a time to meet friends and acquaintances here.

The best reason for going to a good bar is the company you occasionally get, and the company here is the best I have found. You need to have a little patience in the bar; it does not always work. People here care little about status or background. The conversations are steered by what is said and not by who is saying it. We can talk about all kinds of things without being judged according to expectations or stereotype.

Tonight Engle and Bente are working behind the bar, while Rune is in the kitchen. They are just as good company as the guests. When Rune is doing the cooking I always order a chili burger. His salsa is so good that I ask for a double helping.

Christer works in IT; Espen is a rigger for concerts and events. I am not quite sure what Johan does, even after chatting with him in the bar many times over the years. He works at Oslo and Akershus University College as a caretaker or a lecturer. I sit down beside them. We fall into conversation about work, about books, all kinds of crap.

Snorre, a Danish carpenter employed by a large firm, appears. We share a common occupation but work on two different planets. I have my loft and renovation projects; he works on large construction sites in the city center. Moreover, I run my own business—that is the biggest difference. Our planets follow different orbits but sometimes come close. We both have carpenters' hands and when the wind is high, sending up clouds of dust, we feel the bite of the cold.

Snorre is in his work clothes; he lives a fair distance away and could not be bothered going home to change before coming out again. When he gets through his front door, into the warmth after a week spent in the wind between bare, windowless, concrete walls, it is a shower and sofa that is needed. So if he wants to come here he has to make a beeline from work, because beer and company are also important and the shower and sofa can wait. Snorre and I agree that the milder weather, 14°F to 17°F, at the end of this week was nice, that minus 4°F was a bit much, so it is an improvement, although the wind is just as bad.

A guy comes to the bar to order. He looks at Snorre, and upon noticing what he is wearing, says: "Come straight from the job, have you? Still in your work clothes?"

He is obviously in high spirits and feels like cracking a joke. I am half-expecting him to give Snorre a nudge in the ribs. He makes a quip about Danes drinking Bavarian beer at lunchtime.

"How does that work out in the afternoon then—are the meters and centimeters still the same length?"

Ah yes, Danish tradesmen drinking on the job, that old chestnut, no beating around the bush. Snorre first looks at him and then over at the group of people he was sitting with. He motions with his thumb over his shoulder.

"And you lot, payday pint is it?" he says, which it obviously is. "In your work clothes? You all look so alike, I mean. Is there a dress code at the office or what?"

This time he does wait for an answer. The guy is perplexed. Snorre lets the question hang in the air, before turning back to the rest of us. The guy gets his beer, returns to his table, and we are left to ourselves again.

"Was I a bit arrogant?" Snorre says.

Maybe, but that guy certainly was, without realizing it.

If someone is going to take the mickey out of a Danish trades-man and his drinking it is us, his mates, and not an ironic office worker adhering to a dress code he is not even aware of.

We continue to chat and the conversation turns to the construction business. Those working in it now may not be models of health but there was a lot more drinking in the old days, and being the oldest, I tell a few yarns about the empties I had to clear away when I started out and how people drank on the job in the 1980s. We talk about these things, without any particular reference to drunken Danes.

Times have changed, and nowadays you seldom hear of anyone being tipsy on scaffolding or high while operating dangerous machinery. Yet I wonder what happened to those people, if they are still around, or if they are out in the cold, incapacitated, dead. Sobriety in society overall has not increased, so either they have quit working life or changed their drinking patterns and now stay clean on the job. I think there are many explanations, but one of them is to be found in the statistics for long-term sick leave, and if that is the case, it is safe to say that society has become less tolerant, since there is less space for these people in normal daily life.

The mere thought of a drunk with a circular saw makes me shudder, so I have zero tolerance for drinking on my work sites. Not wanting people drinking on the job is one thing, but excluding people completely, in order for the whole thing to run more smoothly, comes at a price. Daytime drinking is only one example. This also applies to other aspects of society where what was previously regarded as acceptable is now viewed as problematic. Streamlining gives rise to intolerance on the personal level and individuals become squeezed between rules and authority. This results in many people not working, since giving 70 percent is not enough; everyone needs to be operating at 100 percent. The fact that that percentage varies a lot for many of us does not seem to matter very much.

All the same, I am glad not to run the risk of stashed empties landing on my head every time I lift a ceiling tile, as was the case on building sites in the 1980s.

Snorre tells us about the construction site he is currently on, along with two or three hundred other employees. The working languages are Norwegian and English, in all possible variants and at all levels, as well as sign language.

Snorre shows us a sheet of paper he has taken from one of the work huts, copies of which hang on all the shower doors. Apparently the water pipes run under the huts, and the water in them can freeze. The sign says, "let the water run in the shower," in Norwegian at the top and in nine languages underneath. A German has commented, in German, that his language is absent. Someone else has corrected the Icelandic, making it into a full sentence. Icelanders are renowned for being particular about language.

The point Snorre is trying to make is that it is not only in oil and IT you find an international workforce in open-plan offices, albeit his place is probably more open-plan than most, considering the wind that has buffeted him all week. He argues that this linguistic diversity also demonstrates broad-mindedness and tolerance, and he is probably right. That half-finished office block is a Tower of Babel. This diversity has practical consequences, not least on language.

A large part of the jargon of all our professions is of foreign origin and has become a natural part of our own everyday speech. Our language has been enriched, but will the labor migration we are witnessing have a similar result? Will we,

LA VANNET RENNE I DUSJEN

Let the water run in the shower

Anna veden valua suihkussa

Leiskite vandeniui bėgti į dušą

Puść wodę pod prysznicem

Пустите воду в душе

讓我們在淋浴水運行

Låtið vatnið Renna

ÙR Krananum í sturtunni

Deje correr el agua en la ducha

Und wo steht das auf Deutsch?

instead of German and English words, import Polish and Lithuanian words into our language?

In practice, linguistic differences can be tricky to deal with. On large construction sites in particular, the use of technical terminology has declined. Often the workers have a hard time understanding one another. This is only intensified by the tangle of contractors, with their varying pay and working conditions. Workplaces are split linguistically, culturally, professionally, and socially.

In my area of the building trade, on smaller projects, it is much the same, albeit on a modest scale. One unfortunate effect of language problems is that many of those running smaller contracting firms often do not comprehend Norwegian well enough to read and understand drawings and specifications. They operate to a large extent on guesswork based on experience in choosing ways to approach the building process. The experience they have is sometimes limited. It can lead to some very odd solutions.

For many foreign tradesmen, running their own company might mean the realization of a dream of independence of sorts, or else simply a way of getting a job. They invoice at a low hourly rate, but it is still something, better than nothing, or more than what they could invoice for in whatever country they come from, as the phrase has it. The motivation lies in just keeping it going, and good quality handwork is not always so easy to deliver in those circumstances.

That this should prove problematic in many cases is hardly surprising, but there is no telling how it will be viewed fifty years from now. The linguistic side of the discussion around labor migration, and immigration in general, has many facets.

Artisanal traditions go far back in time, and on the outskirts of Europe, where I find myself, the milieus were so small that we had to learn from larger technical environments, from industries like mining, shipping, and shipbuilding, from workers in metal, textiles, and construction. Craftsmen traveled abroad to learn and we brought specialists here to our shores. We have learned a lot from others. That was normal and remains so.

The terminology followed the trades. The struts to be removed from the loft in Torshov are called *strevere* in Norwegian. A *strever* is also a careerist, an opportunist. The word is part of our common professional parlance and comes originally from the German *streber*. It is related to "strive"—to contend and struggle—and arrived, in all likelihood, in the same way that new words come now, with the workers. And there are many striving in the construction industry. The competition that arises, increasingly a natural part of working life, turns those participating into people who strive, who contend and vie. It is behavior resulting from the ruthlessness we see in the city's Tower of Babel and that can probably be called terminological irony.

9

JON PETERSEN CALLS TO TELL ME THAT ONE OF THE
contractors needs more time. Accordingly, they have delayed
the deadline for sending in bids until three weeks from Friday.
I have received the new drawings and calculations for the
roof construction and based on those I assume the plans will
be approved. It is a pretty safe bet. Getting my tender offer
finished in time should not be a problem now.

On Tuesday I go to the site to look it over with my people—
the bricklayer, painter, electrician, metalworker, HVAC specialist, and plumber. The electrician and plumber arrive at 11 a.m.;
the others are coming at noon.

Finn, the plumber, has swapped the building site for an
office. He prices jobs and manages projects. Who actually
comes to carry out the work at a site can vary, but the firm has
few employees, so whoever it is, I will know them. It is a pretty
common career path for tradesmen, winding up in an office
and becoming part of the apparatus needed to run the administrative part of a company. For some it is a conscious choice,
understood from the time they start in the business. They serve
an apprenticeship or study for a qualification, then work for
a time in the field in order to gain practical experience before
going on to further education. There are courses organized

within the sector providing opportunities to go to technical college or attend university for a few years. Finn has no formal education beyond a certificate of apprenticeship, but he has a lot of practical experience, and he is good at pricing and dealing with customers.

Some find they can no longer tackle the physical demands of the work. They wear out their shoulders and back and are forced to change jobs, but continue with what they know in another form. There are many who cannot endure this work over a period of years. Injuries, particularly from wear and tear, are often permanent, and do not disappear following time off or an operation. That kind of damage afflicts you for the rest of your life.

When discussion about these types of injuries comes up someone will more often than not opine that all occupations have their difficult sides. This is no doubt true, but usually the person saying this does not have a physically demanding job, and will go on to relate how much stress and psychological pressure there is in his or her work situation. The implication being that physical work is pleasant, uncomplicated, and we get to see the results of our labor. While it ought to be obvious, it is worth stating that manual work does not function as a panacea against stress or conflicts with your coworkers.

The quota of administrative positions in the construction trade is low and many people are simply forced out of the business. If a post for a project manager opens up, a newly educated engineer, not a seasoned tradesman, will usually get the job. An academic background is frequently preferred to a practical one, even where the organization of practical work is concerned.

No matter how you look at it, one consequence of the

dropout rate among skilled tradesmen is that the business is being drained of knowledge. People are quitting when they are at their best, when their experience is ample and their skills honed, at the stage when they are a source of expertise.

Ebba has come to take a look at the electrics. It is not often you meet women on building sites. In that sense she is an exception. She is also competent, prompt in her estimates, and punctual.

While having a look around, we all do a quick run-through of the project. I ask if there is anything they notice that we should pay particular attention to and they in turn come with any questions they have. They each get a copy of the sections of the tender documentation they need. We agree as to when they should have their estimates ready and that I will call them after I have had a chance to look through what they send me.

The painter views the property and takes notes, counts the number of corners, the total area in square feet, and the skirting, casing, and trim in feet. I ask him for a price with standard paint and for one that is more expensive and more durable. The quality of paint varies a lot and I reckon it is a nice little cherry on top of the bid to show that we are thinking of everything. Producing an alternative price does not take much time. We agree on what kind of covering they will require during the work. I will wait as long as possible before putting down the floor, until most of the plastering and painting has been carried out. That means less covering and, more important, less chance of damage to the floor.

There seems to be something in Vietnamese culture that stimulates people to paint. It is the trade in which most of them are to be found. This theory is based on my own meager statistical findings. Tam is quick at everything he does and speaks his own private version of Norwegian, so it can be hard to understand everything he says. Still, he does a good job and his prices are all right. I am not quite sure what kind of professional background he has but he is good at his job and strict in the quality assessment of what his firm delivers.

It smells delicious when the painters are at work because they make hot food for lunch. They bring along rice cookers and prepare all kinds of vegetables and sauces. It reminds me of being on trips in the woods and setting up camp. The smell of hot food is not very common on building sites.

Petter is the sheet metal worker who my old boss used, from back when I was still learning the trade. He is a funny guy and good at his job. Petter is a tonic, and what I should really do is arrange site meetings with him on days I need cheering up. We have cooperated on so many jobs that figuring out the practical details never takes long and more often than not we wind up talking about angling. We both like fly-fishing and trout, but I find his penchant for pike incomprehensible.

Petter is going to give me a quote for ventilation, and a few covers for ducts and a soil pipe that will be led up through the roof. In addition I ask him to price some repairs on the existing ventilation. This is not in the specifications and will fall under the heading of extra work. Best to do it while he is here and get it out of the way. I always ask Petter to take a look at the original metalwork to check if everything is in order. He pops his head out of the old roof window to see if the chimney stacks are in good condition. Some of the flashings are covered by snow, but what he can see looks fine. We chat a little more about ice fishing and then we are all done.

Next it is the bricklayer's turn. Scratch-coating walls, chimneys that need repairing, and a bathroom floor to be poured and tiled. The bricklayer, Johannes, is also an old acquaintance. We know one another through work and have no contact beyond that; all the same I think of us as friends.

I owe my livelihood to them, to the jobs they have given me, and vice versa.

We have shared anxious moments, stood together when money has failed to materialize and bills needed paying, and we have been tired and had to pep one another up when jobs needed doing, and doing properly. Shortcuts are not acceptable. But we have never needed to speak harshly to one another; that is probably another reason why we get on.

I never feel a greater pride in my profession than when carrying it out alongside people like these. I know them like I know no one else, in a way I could never adequately explain to anyone other than others like us. They feel the cold, suffer the dust, the same as I, and have a good understanding of what I do. The mutual respect we have would be difficult for outsiders to understand. This cooperation is one of the best things about being a craftsman.

10

THE TENDER DOCUMENTATION IS SO GENERAL THAT I
have to separate my calculations, itemize them in order to
obtain an overview of the major parts of the job. I can then
check each item as I go. There are spreadsheets for this
purpose but I have never learned how to use them, even if they
would probably be more convenient. A job of this type is not so
easy to work out anyway, as it calls for a fair amount of personal
assessment of the various items. Calculation programs are
not designed with improvisation in mind. It may be more
time-consuming but I do it the old-fashioned way, banking on
my own experience.

I begin by determining quantities, square feet of
floor, plastic sheeting, vapor membrane, insulation, timber per
foot, steel for nailing strips, and so on. I count windows and
doors. I then estimate how many fasteners, how much adhesive and sealant are needed. The materials required for every
single part of the project need to be considered, from when you
start tearing down until the moment you hammer in the last
nail and tighten the last screw.

When I log in to Thaugland Lumber and Builders Provid-
ers' website the prices come up minus my discount. I buy nails,
screws, adhesive, and sealant at Motek. Both businesses focus

on the professional market and it shows. They stock a proper range of products and have knowledgeable people both on the shop floor and upstairs. Not having to wait for hobbyists to finish asking their many questions about the two feet of skirting board they may or may not buy is a welcome consequence of it being builder oriented. As a tradesman it is nice to see people attempt some DIY, but it is a relief to avoid having to stand in line behind them.

The potential shopping list comes to $34,000.

I now need to estimate the amount of waste, and formulate a plan for dealing with the different types of debris: composite and pure wood, plaster, clay, and, in this case, asbestos. I calculate how much it will cost to dispose of the rubbish. There are strict regulations regarding asbestos and I leave the job of clearing that away to specialists. The work itself is not complicated, but has to be done correctly and must be documented. I have removed asbestos myself as an employee when I was starting out, when the well-being of workers was not high on the agenda, but I do not do it anymore.

Asbestos is a nasty mineral, used for its fire-resistant properties, and was installed even in ordinary residential housing. When I think about how strict the regulations are today it makes me wonder how many cases of cancer there have been among tradesmen over the years. The people who manufactured and sold asbestos denied the dangers, even long after these were widely accepted. It is often the way with that type of product and the parallels with the tobacco industry come to mind, or the use of mercury by dentists, where dental assistants spent years litigating to prove their case.

Building sites are full of dust from waste, insulation, wood, and sheet materials. And then there are all the chemicals previously used and those still in use. Solvents in glue and painting products, the highly alkaline substances in cement products. Swedes who come to Norway are not accustomed to working with oil-based paint without protective breathing equipment; the rules surrounding this are a lot stricter in Sweden and the EU than in Norway. I have tried to explain to proponents of oil-based paint that white spirits is a powerful greenhouse gas when it evaporates. Just imagine what working with the vapors from painting with that year after year does to you.

Asbestos is a clear example of how hazardous a dust can be, and we still lack sufficient knowledge of the effects of the whole cocktail of chemicals and dust which workers are being exposed to. Cancer and COPD may not seem as dangerous as a fall from scaffolding or an injury sustained by a saw, but they are insidious threats.

When they were constructing the apartment block in Hegermanns gate they used about twenty different materials. Nowadays the building trade uses around fifty thousand different products. That gives you an idea of how complicated it is to obtain an overview of all the substances you come into contact with.

I estimate how long each separate stage of the work will take, the time required to move the storage rooms, put down the floor, make the stairwell, put holes in for windows, lower the ceiling, and get materials in place. All the work hours need to be included; times goes quickly, and labor accounts for approximately 70 percent of the costs on a job like this.

I have developed a good system for lifting materials and lowering debris to limit the time and effort in lugging things up and down stairs. It is dependent upon storing the materials being brought up to the loft in a smart way. The volume is surprisingly large. So much so, in fact, that we will need to use a crane three times during the building process; otherwise the materials would fill up so much space in the loft that working would become impractical. This is a part of the job I like; it requires being methodical, as in a chess game.

When all the sums are totted up, I add an entry for anything unforeseen that may arise, which it will, no matter how thorough my number crunching. It might be something I have overlooked, but it also offsets the optimistic approach I have to my work. That optimism makes it easy to calculate too little time for a job. I am aware of this, so the inclusion of unforeseen costs is a reminder to myself in accounting form. I add 10 percent to the total price and will reduce that percentage at a later stage if I feel secure in my arithmetic.

I include a rough estimate of what my subcontractors will cost. Later, when I have their offers in hand, I can substitute those figures for what they give me and land on a more accurate sum. For the moment, I use figures from previous projects as my guide. The bid will come to approximately $146,000.

This figure is the most important, the one that actually means something, but there is no harm in checking to see if I am way off the mark. I make a few reference totals for comparison.

The most important comparative figure is obtained by a simple calculation where I multiply the total area by a square foot price. To find the cost per foot squared I have to consider how complicated the job seems. When using figures from past experience I need to think about any recent price adjustments and alter my estimate accordingly. A few years ago material prices jumped three times in the space of a year. Those who did not allow for it took a real hit, and a number of firms went out of business. The Petersen job is complicated and warrants a high price per foot squared, particularly since there is a bathroom to take into account. I multiply the figures and arrive at a result.

A third total is obtained by taking the bathroom out of my calculations, or rather placing it in a column of its own at $32,000. Then I recalculate at an average square foot price and add on the bathroom.

I have three figures to compare to my initial total. I can begin to relax a little; the total I arrived at is probably about right.

If I get the bid wrong it is my wages that disappear. Everything after cost of materials, fixed costs, and payment to subcontractors is income, what I live off. Calculating incorrectly can prove expensive. This is a skill in itself, a judgment call, an estimate, so a 10 percent variation is not much in relation to the total, but in my case it amounts to a loss in revenue of $15,000.

I have completely miscalculated bid tenders in the past. One time I ended up with $2,400 in taxable income and I had worked particularly hard that year. At least there was some consolation in knowing I did not need to worry about tax arrears the following autumn, but I was paying almost $13 an hour from my own pocket to do that job. You live and learn. Providing you get the math right.

My old boss told me he grew anxious every time he won a bidding round. He would start to wonder if he got the job because he had priced himself too low.

I have now worked out both the renovation and carpentry

needed for the job. The renovation is construction work: plastering, putting in windows, and other larger jobs. Carpentry is setting up door and window casing, trim and skirting boards, fitting interiors, finer work. I carry out both types of labor and do not regard carpentry as harder than renovation work. In the case of a loft, I happen to think the opposite is true, but it always depends on the type of work you are talking about, and how practiced you are in the different tasks. The tension between the two thought processes involved is professionally challenging. I have to think about finish when building rough. What I do in January needs to be thought through so the work on the finish is feasible and looks good in May.

In Norwegian culture it is normal for a tradesman in the construction business to have knowledge of an entire job, of his whole field. The definitions of our trades are much broader than in many other cultures. In other parts of the world, tasks are to a larger extent divided between different trade groups and each individual worker has a much narrower spectrum of competence.

Mundane labor has little prestige in any trade and it is often dismissed as donkey work, but that part of the job is actually the test of whether you are a competent, hardworking tradesman, or a slouch. The tradesman who strips something down and prepares it properly for the next stage is likely to be good at the rest of his job.

People with practical jobs like cooks, carpenters, farmers, and fishermen share this simple, fundamental attitude to their work. You cannot be competent and put on airs at the same time, be too good for your own job. In general, training in a craft follows a development from basic work to finer work. It also tells you something about someone's psyche if they view groundwork as donkey work, or if they see it as an obvious, essential part of the job.

It also says something about the society we live in. The fundamentals of production are being further and further removed from sight. We know less and less about it. We shield ourselves from noise and dirt, and our attitude toward practical work is another example of this distance.

The consequences of simplifying the work craftsmen carry out are more complicated than the obvious, rational thoughts about efficiency. Sales brochures are like sterile caricatures of our lives; the production is not shown, and neither are those who produce the goods, and by this I mean the workers, the ones who make the objects. We do not want dirty work; we want a simple and cheap end product.

This perception of production means that working, in the sense of becoming dirty and physically tired, is not deemed a good thing. Ideally this type of work is to be avoided. The relocation of production to controllable environments, factories, is a natural consequence of this ideal. The next step is physically moving this reality away, transferring it to where labor is cheaper, and where people have to put up with working conditions unthinkable to us. The work cannot be carried out more efficiently or get much cleaner than that, as far as we are concerned.

But craftsmanship can never be clean and sterile, as images of the final product would have us believe. When something is manufactured elsewhere, in China, for example, it is out of sight and therefore out of mind. It does not mean that the work is clinical or pure, as the pictures in the brochure would suggest; it is just so far away we do not see it.

In Norway, discussion about building tends to focus on new

structures. They are presented in slick prospectuses, where trees and people soften their visual impact. New buildings also require real workmanship, even though their construction is often simpler and cleaner than in the case of restoration.

The structures already standing, however, represent the bulk of the buildings in the future. We can find new, more effective ways of renovating and modernizing these buildings but it is impossible to do that in a sterile environment where dirt, cold, and sweat do not occur. And who would be willing to do those kinds of jobs if building is considered to be dirty work?

The discussion around "passive housing" is a good example with regard to this. The definition of a "passive house" is, like all other building standards and technical regulations, a changeable one. Just as it has always been. To most people, reducing an ecological footprint in this way sounds beautiful but complicated. But in reality it is easier to accomplish than renovating an older house. And yet renovation has this ordinary, dirty air about it, making it less worthy to talk about than passive housing and modern technology.

If efforts are to be made in relation to energy efficiency in a building market under pressure, then they ought to be directed toward the renovation of existing buildings. Insulating new buildings in a slightly better way has less significance for energy consumption than renovating the buildings we already have.

For politicians it is easier to sound more credible when speaking about a standard passive house than about the large, varied building projects that maintenance and upgrading invariably cover. One simple example is more marketable, politically, than having to explain a complex situation.

Meeting all the challenges this presents requires a different focus on craftsmen and on the work they do. At least if the challenges are to be met effectively.

Words are carefully chosen; customers have to justify their choices, and individuality is put back into the products by calling them *design*. When the individual element in the very production of something disappears, it has consequences beyond the workers it directly affects. Choices with regard to quality and customization soon dwindle when products are made on the far side of the globe. To believe you can remove individuality from the production process and then find it again in the finished product is unrealistic.

It is craftsmanship itself that needs to be given space. And if this space is provided then we can expect things to be made that each of us will think are beautiful and functional. Yes, and some of the things will be ugly, or stupid, and then we will have something to talk about.

Diversity is part of the nature of craftsmanship. The possibility of getting objects made is the most important tool of designers. If we have lots of talented designers and no one to actually make the things, then what do we sell? Maybe we could export designs and ideas, or maybe we could simply export the designers.

11

I HAVE SUBMITTED BIDS FOR THREE LARGE JOBS OUT to tender recently and I have lost all three. That means I have used up a lot of time trying to get work, so I am both fed up and just a little desperate. Smaller jobs, like the one in Kjelsås, are not enough to provide a liveable income, so larger projects are needed regularly.

I have to be careful not to allow my desperation to show. In my dealings with the Petersens, I display a mixture of distance and enthusiasm. If I come across as too keen to win the contract then it may seem as though I have problems getting jobs.

With regards to my Eastern European colleagues, the general view would appear to be that their desperation is taken for granted, is even a competitive advantage, given of course that this desperation is reflected in their prices. We all need to conform and adapt according to our walk of life, our nationality. The nuances are subtle and sophisticated, like red wine. We should not have too fine a bouquet; the taste should be rounded and distinct, with the briefest of aftertastes, like the unobtrusive memory of a good job. A mild, spicy, eccentric aroma is fine, but it must be pleasing.

The phrase "Polish tradesman" in marketing terms implies, at best, a somewhat lower price than I can offer. The automatic expectation of something being cheap based on nationality should in any case evoke in the customer a slightly unpleasant, bitter aftertaste.

On the first of the three contracts I was beaten fair and square, losing on price. I know people in the firm that landed the job and got to hear, openly and honestly, what the other contractors had bid.

If the client allows good firms to compete on a level playing field in tender rounds then the prices do not vary a great deal. Losing out in that way is almost encouraging, since it means my price was close to the one chosen and my calculations were not far off the mark. Maybe next time I will be the one who wins.

As regards the second job that was out to tender, I have no idea on what basis the clients made their choice. I did not even know they had made a decision until I rang up to ask and found out I had not got the job. That happens occasionally and is not particularly pleasant.

The last contract out on tender was also a loft renovation and I got to hear what had happened quite by chance through an acquaintance. He was, it turned out, a friend of the client, and found his behavior so objectionable he felt the need to tell me.

The client had in this case already decided upon a contractor and was only out to adjust the price should it prove necessary. The invitation to tender was carried out with an agreement already in place between the client and contractor, both of whom knew one another. In this instance both I and another carpenter were used to gauge the prices, but neither of us had any chance of landing the job.

At the moment I am waiting on price proposals from Johannes, Petter, and the others. Petter can be a little tardy so I call him to remind him that I need his offer. It is not a big problem; there never are any when working with Petter, and if he gets the estimate slightly wrong we will sort it out.

The tender is on schedule and Jon Petersen is happy about it; they want to make a start as soon as possible and finish in June at the latest.

I can now pick up where I left off in Kjelsås, put in the last two windows and finish off the decking. I have to shovel and sweep away the snow to get to it, and screw down the planks with cold fingers, with the temperature at 5°F.

The loft in Torshov is becoming more important with every day that passes, or rather with every day of employment I use up. I consider getting in touch with some carpenters I know to inquire if they have any work going. I could also ring my old boss or ask the Association of Master Builders to send an SMS to all their members informing them a master carpenter is available for work.

Asking colleagues for work is not ideal when you are uncertain whether you will actually have the time to turn up, which I will not if I get the job in Hegermanns gate. If I win the bid I would have to get going immediately. The time frame on a project like this rules out dropping things to carry out other jobs. Steady progress is absolutely necessary both in order to finish on time and to maintain a good relationship with the Petersen family.

This is the constant predicament, because you want to say yes to job offers. Turning down customers is bad for your reputation. You always have to weigh what you are capable of doing against the principle of not saying no, and that means it can be hectic at times. You are always working with the thought at the back of your mind that one day there might not be enough work.

12

IT IS NOT UNCOMMON FOR A CLIENT TO PRESENT YOU with a partially completed contract. This can be fine at the outset, but all the details matter, so I am in the habit of making an overview of what I believe should be contained within an agreement.

I state how long the offer is valid for and the date it is possible to start and specify the time required for the building period. These clauses are open to discussion and I write that down too. The offer can be adjusted according to possible price changes from the time the contract is entered into. I also include some points about storing of materials, disposal of waste, and other issues.

The proviso about satisfactory drawings and an engineer's calculations being available at all times is slightly farcical. It is a little odd that it does not go without saying, but obtaining detailed drawings can be tricky in many cases. I regularly experience an architect letting out a heavy sigh, telling me I can figure it out, as though it is a compliment, my being able to do their job as well as they can.

I do not ask for drawings merely to do the job. Having documentation of the solutions chosen and being able to assign responsibility for the plan is just as important. I want to cover my back.

One of the conditions I include in contracts is a system of fixed daily fines in the event of delayed completion. The clients appreciate it and feel it means I take deadlines seriously, which I do anyway. The most important thing for me is that the daily fines are foreseeable and cheap compared to the alternatives.

Should the client have any grievances, a lack of clarity in the agreement at the outset can easily lead to a dispute, which in turn may lead to legal proceedings. That can become an expensive process—particularly if the ruling is compensation for inconvenience caused, which can be a considerable lump sum, as opposed to a fixed amount per day.

In the worst cases the outcome of a dispute is that the client need not pay the final invoice in full; the cost is divided, with the client only being required to pay half. The courts want to find a ruling that both parties can accept, not necessarily ones we like.

Conflicts can arise over the time used, solutions chosen, or the level of workmanship. The possibilities are many. One thing is for certain. Becoming involved in a dispute can keep you awake at night for weeks or months. The time it takes up and the worry it causes is often a lot more costly than lawyers' fees.

From a legal standpoint, in any relationship between the tradesman and the customer, we are the professional party and should know best. Running a small business, it is difficult to have an overview of all the legislation that might affect my job. My legal department is rather modest compared with those of the larger contractors. Clearly I should know more about the law than my average customer, but smaller firms also encounter very capable private individuals who have a pretty flexible relationship to laws and contracts.

I am of the view that the law represents a minimum code of good behavior and things should not be taken to extremes at every opportunity. For some clients it is more natural to let these disagreements be worked out by lawyers than it is for the tradesman. The number of clients with family lawyers increases the farther west in Oslo you go. Customers with a low threshold for calling their lawyers are best avoided. The actual wording of the laws can be fairly vague in many instances. Here is one example from the law governing supply of goods and services:

Paragraph 5, Section 1; (1) The service provider will carry out the service professionally in addition to
(2) attending to the client's interests with reasonable and due care.
To the extent the conditions require, the service provider will advise and consult with the consumer.

What does *professionally* mean? *Due care* can cover any number of things. It is not unlikely we may have different opinions on what constitutes care and how reasonable it should be. *Extent* is a fundamentally relative concept. The same goes for *advise* and *consult*.

A lawyer I know quoted me an expression used in legal circles in Norway: "being right is free, proving you are right is expensive." In a dispute, if the sum in question is in the region of $10,000, you have to ask yourself how much you want to be proved right. Most arbitration ends up with a settlement of half the original amount and many tradesmen will not even pursue these to the end. The inconvenience caused and legal expenses incurred are not worth $5,000, and that gives you some idea of what a burden these kinds of cases can be.

So it is assumed that the professional party in question, the tradesman, knows best. It is not so easy to know what is best when judgment enters into the picture, or to know when the client does not fully understand the consequences of particular choices.

The clients may not have specialist or technical knowledge, but in some cases they do not spend any time acquainting themselves with the build itself. They behave almost as if they are buying a finished product in a shop, like a television or a coat.

In many cases customers are downright difficult, and win a case in that manner. The tradesman's professionalism is used against him, as he should know his field, he should have the answers, while customers are usually regarded as babes in the wood.

Many tradesmen have the impression of being fair game for clients wanting to exploit legislation to their advantage. Be difficult and you win, and if you have a family lawyer you win more.

The worst is getting bogged down in a dispute with friends or family you have done a job for. I have made the mistake myself of basing a job on a verbal agreement because I knew the customer well. We were close friends. That friendship ended in a sad way.

13

RENOVATION OFTEN ENTAILS WORK BEING CARRIED out in a different order than would be practical when building from scratch. If I win the Petersen bid, the subcontractors will work at an hourly rate, as well as having a markup on materials. Tam paints for a fixed price, which suits both parties.

When I organize a project in this way, work can be carried out in the most logical sequence. There is more room for improvisation and that allows for more practical, sometimes smarter solutions.

Paying by the hour can result in wild, uncontrolled costs. Making it work requires a clear overview of the entire process, as well as good cooperation between capable professionals. Carpentry touches upon all the other professions, so it is natural that the carpenter administer the build. The carpenter's field is versatile and thus at the heart of renovating a loft like this.

The deal with the client being fixed-price means I can organize the job as I want, and bank on cooperating with my subcontractors based on the confidence I have in them. I am the one taking all the risk, but if it goes well I get a larger profit.

Traditionally, craftsmen used to cooperate directly on

building sites without too much interference from an administrative level above. This flat structure without too many managers, but with good communication between those producing, is the natural form of cooperation among craftsmen. This model is becoming more and more of an ideal than a reality in the day-to-day business of the building trade. Formalities are becoming increasingly more important and the direct responsibility resting on each individual has become much less clear. This is perhaps one of the reasons that red tape seems so necessary. One form of collaborative culture is being replaced with another form, a culture of monitoring. This supervisory control is to a large degree not even based on real control, but on forms and indirect checks through paperwork.

You must first tick a box to indicate you understand something is important and subsequently tick a box when it is done. What you make only assumes its value when the ticks have been checked over by another person. This has to be done because management are not around when they should be, are not present to answer questions and make decisions. It is a system where responsibility is to all appearances precisely assigned but in practice is not taken. This is a caricature of the situation but not that far removed from how many workers perceive it.

The trend in the relationship between different types of tradesmen is similar to what is happening between tradesmen and architects, engineers and clients. It is a dramatic shift in our building culture.

There are several reasons why building companies choose to go along with this bureaucratization of their own industry. Document-based quality control pervades all areas of society and tradesmen can hardly be exceptions. Larger firms have a lot of power, and anyway they have administrative departments ready to tick boxes and have therefore little reason to oppose such a system. The smaller firms are the ones who lose out, since this way of working does not particularly suit them. In this manner, larger companies gain a competitive advantage.

I have received the subcontractors' quotes, so my calculations are now complete. Petter has given me an oral estimate that I have used for the metalwork. There are no big surprises and when everything is totted up the total bid comes in approximately as expected, at $143,000.

I have also included an estimate for extras. These figures are based on simple descriptions of work I believe ought to be carried out, but they are not included in the tender documentation.

I take one last look through the numbers and then the bid is ready to be delivered. I attach the text where I wrote down the most salient points I want the contract to cover and the conditions governing the bid.

After putting everything in an e-mail and sending it, the best thing I can do is try to forget it until such time as I find out whether I have won or lost the contract. In other words, if I have work for the next six months. In two weeks the Petersens will decide who they want to come in and help build their new home.

14

THE JOB IN KJELSÅS HAS COME TO AN END; THE customer is satisfied and the final invoice has been sent.

I have been asked to do a minor job I had previously been out to look at. I had given up on hearing back from the client when they rang out of the blue and asked if I had time. It means four days in Nordstrand, at an hourly rate with an immediate start, and I am acutely aware of some jobs being worth more than others.

It is a plum job changing kitchen cupboards and work tops for a pleasant customer. They are happy I can start right away. For me it is perfect, I have nothing else on. This is the kind of job that often leads to more work, either from the client himself or from people they know. Years may go by without anything happening, but the finished job remains in place, like a business card. If it is done well, it also acts as a good reference.

I have sent out word that I am available for work, among friends, relations, at the bar, and to my subcontractors. I will wait for the time being before approaching colleagues and possibly getting in touch with the Association of Master Carpenters to have them send out a text.

I take the opportunity to spend a week's holiday on the

south coast, in Sørlandet, my family and childhood home. Food, fishing, sleep, and more sleep. My summer holidays were brief and things have been pretty hectic since. The rest is a tonic, even though it takes me three or four days to stop thinking about work.

Each night before falling asleep my mind runs riot with pointless speculation, drowsy ideas whirling around in all directions. I wake up in the middle of the night and continue with more muddled thinking. Money, bills, technical details, clients and their wishes, round and round its own unstable axis.

Ultimately all this constant pondering is an idiotic way to prove to myself I am not a slouch, and am hardworking. If it all goes wrong then at least I tried, gave everything. When I take time off a space opens up for all these stupid thoughts. Maybe it is because I do not have concrete tasks to concentrate on. It makes room for doubts. It will be good to be rid of them.

An e-mail arrives from the Petersens, and I feel my pulse increase and my heart beat a little faster. I make some coffee, go outside in the cold to sit on the steps, light up a cigarette, and open the e-mail. I do not like things happening fast, nor heights, or anything frightening for that matter. Extreme sports would not be my kind of thing, and neither do I need them— this is excitement enough.

Yes! They would like to use my firm, me. There are some matters they would like to discuss—could we arrange a meeting? Yes, we most certainly can. I am happy, and relieved. This job is going to be good, better than the last, the best ever.

I know I tend to overreact to this kind of news, also when it is bad news and means disappointment. I should be prepared, keep my cool, but it means much in both a practical and emotional sense. It is all tied up together, not having to worry for a while about money, getting up each day and going to work. Being able to afford going on a summer holiday and having reason to take one, tiring myself out and sleeping well, succeeding, if only for the next five months.

When people ask me how it is going I will not have to hesitate before answering, I can explain how things are without complaining or seeming to whine. The question is well intentioned, but it sets me off thinking about so many things. It is as though all my worries emerge with renewed strength each time. At the moment I can happily reply that I have enough to be getting on with, and what is more, it is a nice job.

15

I AM SITTING IN THE PETERSENS' KITCHEN. IT IS A Thursday afternoon in early January and the whole family is home. Kari and Jon are sitting at the table with me and both children are darting around in that state of shy excitement children display when there is an unfamiliar face in the house. I greeted Jens and Fredrik politely when I arrived. Fredrik is the older; he is five and a half years old and Jens is three and a half. Jens was a little wary of me at first, but he shook my hand after Fredrik had done it. I will no doubt become better acquainted with these two boys in time.

Part of our agreement is that the builders can use the kitchen as an eating area. We can have lunch here, get water from the tap, and also use the toilet facilities. I remember how strange it felt the first few times I intruded on people's private lives in this way. I always bring my own towels to keep in the bathroom, although some clients tell us we can just use theirs. We cannot help bringing dirt and dust into their personal area though. As much as possible I try to avoid washing in the customers' sinks. I do not like seeing the grayish-brown water dirtying the white porcelain, and try as I might to rinse it clean I never think it looks as before.

They are impressed that I insist on having daily overrun

penalties in the contract, and in turn I get their approval for the building period to be extended by a week, just to be on the safe side. The completion date is set for mid-June next year.

They also accept the inclusion of a clause whereby should I fall ill for any length of time then the completion date can be put back by a maximum of a fortnight.

Thus we have a clear agreement that allows me ample time to carry out the work and will limit conflict should anything go wrong with regards to the completion date, which falls in good time before they had planned to move into the loft anyway.

Most of the matters we have talked about so far are standard issues, but we also need to discuss the parts of the job not included in the documentation and drawings but that nevertheless need doing. The deal is not in the box until we agree about that work and sign the contract.

The largest unforeseen issue was the roof support, where my idea about the new beam configuration was approved. I have priced this and it already forms an additional element in the bid the Petersens have accepted. The presence of asbestos also comes up, and the solution of outsourcing to specialists is approved.

I work my way down the list. They seem to have expected a negotiation like this and have been sensible enough to make allowances in their budget for contingencies. I am relieved.

I mention that it might be the neighbors' responsibility to fix the ventilation shaft that ends in the attic but that needs to be extended through the roof for fire-safety reasons. I am at pains to make them understand that I do not know who should bear the costs of that work. It is something they need to agree on with the other residents. I do not want to seem as if I am sticking my oar in. It would not be good for me to fall out with the neighbors. I will be viewed as a disruptive element in the apartment building anyway. I do not want to be a party to any arguments or conflict in addition.

Kari and Jon understand that the building process will only prove more difficult for everyone if I am dragged into something that might give rise to bitterness or have negative consequences.

The Petersens also have to decide if they are going to replace the old wiring in the apartment's electrics. The old system is composed of steel piping for lights and sockets and the wiring is within this. The electrician, Ebba, recommends changing these, but it will cost almost $2,000 extra. Having found singed wiring in similar old piping in other buildings, I appreciate her advice. In any case, with so much work to be done on the electrical side the extra cost will not be exorbitant. We agree there is no hurry and that they can put off the decision until a later date.

Now it is the Petersens' turn. They have decided they want to have the opportunity of doing some of the painting and decorating themselves. Their efforts will save them some money and help keep their costs down. That is fine by me. I tell them I think it is a good idea to keep project finances in check in this way and ask only that they give me reasonable notice. It is not a large part of the total price we are talking about and what is most important to me is having control of time and the carpentry end of the job, the part I myself will carry out.

The Petersens want to buy the staircase themselves. Staircases, along with kitchens, seem to have greater significance for people than anything else.

It is a part of the home they want to be personally responsible for, so they can show it to family and friends and say we found this in such and such a way, and it was made by some firm or other that can be identified. It is from Suldal, Hestnæs, Verona, or Munich. A staircase is the heart of the home. You descend it, feeling you are on the way to do something, and the children tear up and down it, clamber over it, and play on it.

I tell them buying the stairs themselves will probably not save them much and that it often ends up leading to complications and difficulties. All the same, it is fine by me; I just need to send an e-mail to the staircase manufacturers thanking them for the quotation and explaining there will be no order after all.

The points they are bringing up now are most likely things they have thought about for a long time, and could have been included in the documentation from the get-go, but this is a negotiation and tactics are part and parcel of that. So the points come in ascending order of difficulty, the most debatable at the end.

Now it is time to let the cat out of the bag. Kari's father works at Maxbo, the builders' suppliers, and they can purchase materials at a reasonable price through him. This is not going to be easy.

I explain that in order to guarantee the quality of what I build, I need to be able to vouch for the quality of the materials I use. My main supplier is Thaugland. I know what I am getting with them, and should any problems arise they are always easily resolved. Thaugland also grant me a good discount and that in turn allows me to offer reasonable prices in my bids.

Jon counters by saying the price he could expect from Kari's father would mean a large saving for them. Is it adherence to gender roles that causes Jon to speak about materials and money, almost on behalf of Kari? It is *her* father who has offered to help them, after all. I also wonder if the father, who works in the business, understands that this arrangement would be difficult for a building contractor to accept.

I explain that the normal markup on materials for me on a project like this is in the region of $4,000. That forms part of my income, but is also payment for ordering and taking care of everything around delivery, problems with goods received, returns, and so on. The issue remains hanging in the air for a while until Jon says he understands, but that they are willing to compensate me to some degree, as the prices on offer to them are so good that they would very much like to take advantage of them.

My working methods on building sites and my knowledge of my suppliers' procedures go hand in hand. I know the drivers at Thaugland and which vehicles I need to order to be able to lift the materials up and into the loft. I am familiar with the retailers I use and can quickly locate what I need without having to spend time looking whenever I need to pick up something in person. This is not only time efficient and re-assuring, it makes the building process run smoother as well.

Thaugland are dependent to a large extent on small contractors like me and they are pleasant to deal with. It is important to feel at ease; the impersonal atmosphere at Maxbo makes me feel small and insecure, but I can hardly use that as an argument.

I explain as well as I can, in as subdued a manner as possible, that I cannot go along with such an agreement. This is plainly difficult for them to accept. The money is no doubt important but they are also being met with a refusal, as well as the fact there is a family dimension, the father. He probably wants to help his daughter out whatever way he can.

But this is not something I can budge on. Well, I might, if it meant running the risk of losing the job, but I intend to stand firm. Fortunately they drop it, but then Jon gets a bright idea. He says that since they are not able to buy from his father-in-law they are losing money, which in effect makes it an expense I am causing them. He says they would like a discount on the total price I am offering—compensation, as he puts it, for the extra costs they will now incur. He is haggling without being aware of it, because he is looking for compensation for something he has brought about. He wants $1,300. He is improvising; I can see that by Kari's expression, she clearly finds the situation uncomfortable.

We are talking about less than 1 percent of the total costs, small change really in the larger scheme of things. I cannot argue that the amount under discussion is so small as to be negligible because then it would have to be so for me too. I cannot make the argument that in that case it would mean $1,300 less in pay for me; they could say that was my problem, that $1,300 is a lot of money to them as well. So I say that the bid I made at the start was accepted; it forms the basis for the talk we are now having and we need to stick to it. Fortunately they let it go.

This discussion marks a shift in our relationship. The seriousness is beginning to show in more real terms than before. For the first time I have shown myself to be someone who thinks about more than roof supports, building, and my clients' wishes. I can also think about myself. Uncomfortable though it might be, it is also important and proper to have been through this so early on. We have established our positions, I hope.

We agree on signing the contract as it stands, but on leaving out the details on work they might do themselves until later, and the subsequent removal of the cost of that work from the price should they do it. As assurance for both parties we attach the points not included in the specs as an addendum to the contract.

By 9:00 we have signed the contract and shaken hands. It has been tiring for all concerned, but now we are over the line and can get down to what this is all about: building. Applications for building permission have been sent in, as has the request for alterations to the roof support. We cheated to save time and sent the papers to the planning department before the final contract was signed. In two weeks I will start on the demolition work and relocation of the storage rooms in the loft.

On my way home I call Dan to tell him everything is finally in order. Dan is a carpenter like me and also runs his own firm. We work for each other when it is convenient.

We are both stubborn and do not give in easily in a discussion, something I like having more than he does. He gets a bit tired of me fussing over details, of never being content with a solution before I understand it. He would rather continue working and solve problems along the way, whereas I grow uncertain if I am unsure about what we are doing. My slightly manic insistence on clarity is balanced by his drive and ability to push us onward. The result being we take one thing at a time but are very thorough. Dan is ready to join me when work on the loft in Hegermanns gate begins in earnest.

16

THE TWO WEEKS IN THE RUN-UP TO THE JOB STARTING
go quickly, with all manner of small matters to be taken care of.

Office work is the scourge of running a small business, a
black hole sucking hours and energy, whose pull only seems
to increase the more you put into it. I now have time at my
disposal to tidy up this year's accounts, put papers in order,
and draw up some basic budgets for the next six months.

I tidy up my storage rooms, check my tools, clean them, oil
them, and repair leads and plugs. I take the hammer drill and
one of the nail guns in for a service at Motek—where I also buy
most of my tools—and also have the leveling lasers calibrated.

Streamlining the organization, you could say.

I check a few things online related to the job at the Petersens, gather brochures, and collate the technical specifications
I will need during the build, but also documentation for when
the job is finished.

I have devised my own simple system of photo documentation. Any photographs I take during the building process I put
in a file and number them along with, wherever necessary, a
simple explanatory text of what is shown. In this way I have
an easy-to-follow illustrated guidebook that also doubles as
documentation of the work I carry out, a copy of which I can

give the customer when the job is finished. Combining the photographs with the paper documentation provides a good overview of the work done and is easily understood by the client.

If you are thinking of buying a place, and the choice falls between two similar properties, of which one has thorough documentation on any work carried out and the other does not, you will in all likelihood opt for the property you know is properly built.

There are computer programs available for this, but I like the simplicity of the process I use, as well as the fact that I came up with it myself. I create a file for the job in Hegermanns gate and put in photographs from the site inspections, and have now documented the starting point of the job.

In Ekeberg I fit a door on a bathroom that Johannes, the bricklayer, has put in. I let him know I landed the job in Torshov so he can pencil it into his plans. I want him on the job as early as possible. In that way we will be finished with dust from the walls and any water spillage before building begins on anything we need to be careful to cover. Thus Johannes can work more effectively and we will save on time and protective materials.

Jon has promised to get in touch with Get, the cable television and Internet company, as well as the telephone people, who both need to reroute their cables in the loft. The cables are attached to the ceiling and along the storage rooms that are to be moved. Trying to get the television and telephone companies to move cables can be frustrating. They work with information technology but do not seem to have the first clue about communication. Jon seems doubtful when I emphasize the need to get in touch with them right away, but he promises to do so.

Ebba puts the loft into her calendar. One of the lads will come out and fix up everything electrical; all they need is a few days' notice, she tells me. A number of wires will need rerouting early on in the project. The floor will be taken up and parts of the electrics for the apartment beneath are running along the joists. Some need moving due to the widening of the hole for the stairs, while new conduits for wiring need to be laid for new outlets in the loft.

The materials I take up have to be placed so as not to be in the way of the work we are going to carry out. Some of them will be situated in the part of the loft we are not renovating, where there are storage rooms and some free floor space. I have been lent a storage room to lock up tools and the like. Based on a list, written in order of importance, I have decided what I want in the first delivery from Thaugland. I am going to take in as much as is practically possible and it is going to be a tight squeeze.

I have put the placement of the different materials on a plan drawing I have made to ensure there is adequate space for everything to be hoisted up.

I e-mail Thaugland the order and book the vehicle and crane. I will also make use of the crane to lower the debris. All the waste has to be placed tidily in the loft after demolition to ensure it can be lowered quickly. Wooden debris goes straight into a skip, as do bags of clay, plaster, and stone. Everything effectively separated. Smaller amounts of waste I gather up, put in the van, and drive to the tip myself.

Dan is going to finish the jobs he has got on and join me in working on the loft when things are well under way. All the same, we meet up one evening after his children have been put to bed, and take a look at the drawings and specifications. It is good for him to get an insight into what the project involves. It means he will be better prepared when he does turn up. Like a cheese that improves when left for a time. The project resides someplace in his mind, and without him needing actively to think about it, a sense of the job slowly develops.

We go through the plans and the specs, while drawing up a list of things we need to remember. In addition, we make what we call an "N.B. List." It includes items of particular importance, some easy to overlook or forget. I have already put together one list, but we make a new one independent of this and then compare the two. Mine could have locked us into one way of thinking; it is easier to catch sight of things I have missed when we start over. This list will stay with us throughout the project. We will cross off items as we complete them, and add new ones that turn up. It is our most important checklist.

17

PRIOR TO ANYTHING BEING LIFTED IN OR OUT BY CRANE, I have a good week of hard work ahead of me in the loft. The board of the housing cooperative has approved the move of some of the storerooms and the demolition of others. It is a week ahead of the start date stipulated by the planning office and I had to promise to restore the storerooms to their previous state if there were problems with the approval. I have been given permission to tear up the flooring under the same condition. It is understandable that I have to promise this and amenable of them to allow me to start. Now I have a job to go to on those days I would not have otherwise had, as well as an extra week added onto the deadline for completion.

To take on jobs like this, a tradesman has to have approval from the authorities, at either a local or national level. That is what it means when it says "approved contractor" on tradesmen's vehicles. I do not have approval from the central agency and must seek it locally for every project requiring it. Local approval is, however, never a problem because I have a master craftsman's certificate, considerable experience, and many previous projects to my name.

Central agency approval was actually a condition for taking part in the tender round, but I convinced them I would get it at the local level and was allowed to participate. This is the approval we are now waiting upon, as well as permission to commence the project itself. General permission has been granted, so everything will work out and there is little risk involved in starting to demolish now.

Jon is having a difficult time with the cable television and telecom companies, so there are a lot of leads in the way. I loosen them cautiously, hanging them in a makeshift manner. I then cut the walls of the storage rooms into suitable sections, like a building kit, and put them together again where the new storage spaces are to go. I mark, measure, and cut.

Jon has informed me that some of the residents are unhappy with the new storage spaces they are getting. The new ones will be constructed according to the required standards and will comply with the minimum measurements stipulated. I am not going to make them too small. I need to take into account that 75 inches is the minimum height permitted. The storage rooms also need to have a sensible design; the residents need to be able to take their things in and out, and there are uprights, pipes, chimneys, struts, and ties to take into account.

The architect's drawings are not exact, which means it is easier to adjust the storage spaces while actually constructing them. I mark out the new storage spaces on the floor, which allows me to check the measurements on a scale of one to one, in life-size dimensions. The building kit I have made from the old storage rooms will then be correct and simple to reconstruct.

The storage rooms must be emptied of their contents before they can be moved. There are things all round the loft, piles of more or less usable furniture, odds and ends, keepsakes, and household utensils. Some residents take the opportunity to tidy up and throw out things they no longer have any use for, while others move everything they have, no matter what it may be.

I am given a glimpse into people's lives, whether they are hoarders and what kind of taste they have, or aesthetic sense, as perhaps it is called. Judging by the items I can guess their ages and speculate about what occupations they have, or had. I help one infirm resident to empty his storage room; it is to my benefit too, as it means I can get on with my work sooner.

Some residents suddenly find pretexts for being up in the loft now that their possessions are on the floor outside the flimsy walls of the storage rooms, as though these items, no matter how insignificant they seem to me, need to be looked after now they are visible. The storage rooms have been locked with little padlocks that could be broken open with one strike of a hammer, and the items within have been lying there for years, but are now viewed as vulnerable and precious.

Other residents show me photographs and objects they have not seen in years, and tell me stories about them, before putting them back in storage for a new period in the darkness. These visits to the loft are pleasant.

When the storage rooms are finished and filled up again, I wrap plastic sheeting around them to prevent any dust getting in over the next few months.

The section of loft I am going to renovate is now empty. I am still not ready to bring in materials though. I pull up planks, pull out all the nails that need to go, take down lights, and remove wiring that could be one hundred years old. I remove clotheslines and the eye screws they hang between. The floor is to be taken up and in those places where it is necessary the old clay between the joists dug up and placed in bags. The feeling of being under way is strong, and dusty.

Nails protruding through the roof boards from outside are dangerous. I tend to forget about them when focused on something else and usually end up walking around with cuts on my scalp and forehead from nails I failed to notice before registering the pain. On the last few loft conversions I have worked on I have chopped off these nails with a saber saw. It is better, because a cut on the head is sore, and if there are a lot of them I look like I have been in a fight. I am not an attractive sight with my hair short and bloody scabs all over my head.

People often tell me I should go to the doctor and get a shot, but as long as there is no excrement from the waste pipe or earth in the cuts I have better things to be doing. I have yet to contract tetanus, or septicemia, for that matter.

If I spent my time worrying about getting hurt it would make every working day a nervy one. Perhaps people's concern about nicks and sores is a result of how seldom they expose themselves to the possibility of these injuries. It is not that I enjoy cuts and bleeding; it is just a natural part of the job.

I could use a hard hat, but that would only make my head bigger, which means banging into things the entire time when working in tight spaces, like under a sloping ceiling. Seeing as any injuries incurred are only superficial I choose not to wear one. A baseball cap is adequate protection, safeguarding against most small nicks and cuts.

Larger wounds or more serious injuries are something else entirely. Just thinking about how close I have come to having an accident can make me nauseated. In the moments after losing control and being too close to the blade of a table saw I have at times had to sit down and breathe out, my hands shaking and my body overcome by a strong physical reaction. I think through why it happened.

Am I tired? Is my mind not on the job? Have I too much to think about? Is the work area untidy? Sometimes I go away from the site, have a cup of coffee, and read for a while. It can be a good idea, doing something not related to work.

My hands are tools in direct contact with the materials and whatever else I work with. When pulling up a floor I wear gloves, but I prefer working with my bare hands when carrying out ordinary carpentry. That results in lots of little nicks and scratches. The newer types of gloves you can buy are fortunately much better to work with than the ones we used to use and it is obvious that younger people in the business are more accustomed to working while wearing them.

My nails are always cut short, thus avoiding splinters and the like beneath the nail. When I do get a splinter that I cannot manage to extract I just wait until the infection is just about right, then soak the hand in warm water and green soap, and pick out the splinter with a needle and tweezers. I have a splinter in my middle finger from a couple of years back that got sealed in and became a lump. It does no harm and I imagine it will vanish of its own accord one day.

The floorboards need to be cut in length in order to fit in the skip. I have a different set of tools for demolition work and use a circular saw. I pull up the floor and place the planks down where they are not in the way of the rest of the preparatory work.

There is a subfloor between the floor joists in old apartment buildings like this, on top of which clay was put in as insulation. I remove this clay where the new stairwell is to be located as well as where pipes are to be laid and space is needed for ventilation. The remainder of the clay still serves its function and will be left as was, perhaps as long as the building stands. When I blow my nose in the shower after days like this, black and gray slimy mucus comes out. When the heat and steam of the shower dissolves the dust in my nose I can blow out some formidable clots. Dust masks help, but they are not airtight.

When the original builders brought the clay up 130 years ago they would have walked up chicken ramps at each floor. These had rungs set in at an appropriate distance to allow them to carry such a load. I have had to carry a lot of this clay down in the opposite direction, on other projects, and still cannot imagine what toil it must have been. Enormous amounts of clay were used during the building boom in Oslo, apartment building after apartment building, year after year.

I eat my lunch down in the kitchen and will continue to do so in the coming weeks. Being in unfamiliar surroundings feels strange, and makes me slightly uncomfortable, especially at the moment, since the job is so dusty, but I have to have a place to eat and it is part of the deal. There will be less dust in time and the Petersens will become accustomed to their kitchen being a tradesmen's canteen, so I will feel more relaxed in the not too distant future. I have brought along my own towels and left them hanging in the bathroom, reducing to some degree the feeling of intrusion.

It is the day before the big day: the materials arrive tomorrow. I began cordoning off a section on the street outside yesterday to make room for the crane truck and the skips. The trestles I put out are made of cleaned planks I have torn out and decorated with red and yellow caution tape. As cars disappear from the street I expand the marked-out area. I have to begin in good time and take the space I need as it becomes available. Two skips and a crane truck require a lot of room. I have been following the comings and goings on the street and noticed that cars are not parked there over long periods. One car did not look like it was used very often so I stuck a note on the windshield. That was a week ago and it was moved yesterday. Sometimes I will have to call up a car's owner and ask if they can move it, but that was not necessary this time.

To take in the materials, I make a hole in the roof where a window is going to be put in. It is larger than what is needed for the window and will remain until the last of the materials is lifted in. I use transparent plastic sheeting to seal the hole and that way we get some daylight.

It requires a certain degree of experience to make absolutely sure a hole like this is sealed, while at the same time it can be opened and closed as the need arises. It would border on nightmarish to lie awake at night when it is raining heavily, while the wind shakes my house in Tøyen, worrying about the covering on a job in a different part of the city, the client ringing on Friday night at 10:10 to tell me water is coming down into the apartment below where I am working. The mere thought is enough to ruin a night's sleep, so I think the job out thoroughly and carry it out carefully.

The hole is reinforced on the underside so we can rest the materials on the edge as they are lifted in. I have made a solid trestle on the floor inside so we can set down the materials securely while we pull them into the attic.

There will be batches of long timber, heavy packs of drywall, all kinds of things that will need to come through the hole. We will carry them from there to where they are to be stored in the loft. I have an idea, so tomorrow we will see if the others think it is a cunning plan.

18

IT IS THE END OF JANUARY, ALMOST THREE MONTHS since Jon Petersen first got in touch. Yesterday we received permission to start. Had the authorization not been granted I would have had to postpone the crane lift; I could not have purchased this amount of materials without being certain that everything was in order.

I don't ask for a deposit; I invoice as the work goes on. This is usually every fourteen days or monthly, depending on materials purchased and how much work has been done; that is, the value of the work, including that done by subcontractors, in terms of hours.

We are out in force on the day of the lift. Dan, Ole, and Bård arrived at 8:00 a.m. on the dot. Dan is experienced and can handle anything, anywhere. Safety is foremost in his mind when working, which is important when dealing with heavy loads, a narrow opening into the attic, and lots to keep your eye on.

Ole and Bård are more or less permanent employees in a demolition firm so they pretty much know their stuff, but can be a bit cavalier. They are from Gamlebyen, the inner city, and are at their best when not hungover. I like them; they are good people, hardworking, and full of humor. Bård has *bull* tattooed across the knuckles of one hand and *shit* across the other. That gives you some idea. They are in fine fettle today, which is a good thing, as well as necessary. I have made it clear that everyone needs to be alert and on the ball; otherwise their involvement would pose a risk.

Over the years I have become more attuned to the possibilities of dangerous situations arising. Whether that is due to anxiety increasing with age, or experience on the job making it easier to spot potential danger is difficult to say. Perhaps it is both.

There is a difference between the risk of an accident when I am working alone, with the saw for instance, and when something is being lifted, with many others around. One difference is that when I am alone whatever happens affects me and nobody else. Another is that there is a greater chance of an unforeseen incident the more people there are, in addition to which these are heavy items we are lifting, high up in the air, so the consequences can be serious.

A few years ago I was taking materials into a loft at one of the blocks in Søndre Åsen in the north of the city and almost fell off the roof, 45 feet down to the pavement. The apartment block in question had a fairly flat roof, approximately a 10 percent gradient, and was clad with zinc. It was winter so the frosty metal was as slippery as ice.

I had knocked up a makeshift platform with a railing, so it was safe enough at the outset, but the driver of the hire crane was lethargic or arrogant, and was not concentrating on what was going on. I was standing on the planks I had secured crosswise up on the roof directing and receiving insulation in a cargo net when the net snagged on the platform I was standing on without the operator noticing. The whole platform began to lift, my fear of heights kicked into overdrive, and all I could think of was that I was going to have to jump into the air and grab hold tightly to the net. Rather that than go crashing down to the street below. At the very last moment the operator realized what was happening and stopped lifting. He lowered it gently down and I crept inside, trembling and shaking, back onto the floor of the loft. When I managed to get to my feet again I poured myself a coffee and went down to talk to him. He was on his toes the rest of the day.

Once I was back up on the roof I put on a harness and attached a line to the chimney as an extra safety precaution, something I should have done anyway. My mistake was in thinking the railing was security enough and I was wrong. It was an experience that still gives me the jitters just thinking about it.

Incidents of that kind have led to my being more decisive when engaged in hazardous work. I have learned to trust in my own judgment and not shy away from speaking up.

The Health and Safety Executive would no doubt say that we should not work under dangerous conditions, but the work is inherently dangerous, especially, for instance, when heights and heavy loads are involved. Danger is a relative term. Accidents will happen and all we can do is try to avoid them as best we can and limit the chances of them coming about. My old boss used to say that accidents are never well planned. They can occur even when you are being careful, but being careful still helps.

Nothing is going to happen when I am in charge—that is the most important thing on every job; that is what occupies my mind. If there are untrained or inexperienced people on-site, even if they are only visiting, I will have eyes in the back of my head. My carping can prove a source of annoyance to people, but there is no way I can be sure where to draw the line: to understand when I need to nitpick and when they know what they are doing. Besides, a lot of people think they are in control because they simply are not aware of the dangers.

No one is going to fall off the roof today; that is rule number one. No one is going to be crushed today, or end up in danger of any kind, and that is also rule number one. I tell everyone this as we gather together on the pavement for a coffee and a quick chat before starting. The most important thing is that we watch out for one another.

The skips for the waste have come, and at 8:30 a.m., Svenn, the driver from Thaugland, arrives with the materials as agreed. We compare the packing list with the order.

Everything is fine apart from the windows not being included in the delivery. There are five of them, and with all the accompanying packaging, that will mean fifteen to twenty trips up the stairs to the attic. The windows are so heavy we need two men to carry each of them. Ah well. We will figure it out. It is not a huge setback; I just took it for granted they would be on the truck. If we need to use legs and the staircase then so be it.

We will be in radio contact during the lifting. Svenn and I agree on the meaning of the messages we will give one another. He will be on the street looking at the building while I am standing in the attic looking in the opposite direction, so left and right can become confusing. Up and down will not present a problem. We also agree that we have plenty of time; there is no need to rush. Should any uncertainty arise about anything we will pause, talk it over, and agree on what to do.

When the load is being lowered through the opening in the roof there is little room. No one can stand directly beneath when the load is hanging in the air because if it sways too much from side to side or catches on anything it can be dangerous. Everything is to be carried out in a nice, calm, controlled fashion; that is the cardinal rule.

It is not often I direct a crane. Svenn is a lot more practiced on his end than I am, so it is a good thing he is patient.

We get under way. A load comes in, debris goes out. A load in, debris out. The crane is never empty-handed.

The skips are to be collected after lunch; they cannot remain standing with sorted waste, because they would soon be filled up with rubbish from the whole district. The presence of a container is the only excuse people nearby need to start tidying up and throwing things out, but a skip with sorted wood becomes twice as expensive to empty when someone has chucked a television or plastic waste into it. Then it is no longer sorted. One container for untreated wood, and one for clay and stone. All the bags of clay have to be cut open and their contents emptied into the skip. Plastic is put aside to be driven to the tip later. As long as waste is sorted according to source material from the start, from when I begin demolition, then recycling is not time-consuming. Rather, it contributes to everything being tidier and therefore saves time.

Svenn attaches the straps to the packages on his own and needs no help. Bård, Ole, and Dan take turns running down to loosen what we send down and put it in the skips, then return and assist in placing the materials where they are to stand. They also help Svenn in packing the load to be hoisted in the net: tools, insulation, fasteners, adhesives, what have you. Up and down all day.

The most laborious job is moving everything to where it is to go in the attic. Chipboard for the floor and drywall for the firewall. Batches of heavy timber, 2×8s, 2×9s. A stack of 2x4s along with some other various sizes. The laminated wood beam we rest on top of the collar beams. That proves heavy going, but with four men lifting we manage to get it up.

The insulation for the floor has been placed on planks I have put down across the collar beams in the section of the loft where the storage rooms are. Tools and accessories are placed in the storage room. The skylights and all their related components, well, they are yet to be delivered.

The placement of items in the little loft is based upon the sequence of work tasks and which materials are needed when, how much all the various stacks weigh as well as how much space they take up.

We spend the entire day lifting up and down and loading and unloading. We keep at it, only taking a break to eat. It is heavy going but the sight of the volume of materials accumulating is a good one.

Svenn lifts up the last load of materials, the one with the heavy timbers, the 2×8s, and so on. These are what I will use first, so they are placed in the center of the floor.

Svenn folds the crane back down onto the truck. The others pull in the last batch of materials while I go down and have a quick chat with Svenn and thank him before he finishes for the week.

One of the nicest things I can say about another person is that we have done some heavy lifting together, and I mean that literally. To hold one end of something heavy and be aware of another's movements, feel them transmitted through the object, is an experience all its own. I can tell if the other person is adept at carrying, if they show me consideration or just think of their own burden, and I can sense when they are getting tired. Fatigue is reflected in their step, in imprecise motions. It is expressed by silence. Anyone who is able ought to lift something together with another person from time to time; it is a good way to get to know one another.

Physically, lifting is uncomplicated in that it is directly experienced as weight, as pounds. While doing it you avoid thinking too much about what is around you, what is irrelevant in that moment. It is important to keep in mind that what is heavy is different for all of us. When carrying together, we cannot take more weight than the weakest of us can manage; two people are as one.

Another scenario is when several people lift something really heavy together. For example, four people lifting a ridge beam. You are at the mercy of each other; if one person lets go, another can be injured. Small comments are made the entire time, messages given, adjustments made. We need to talk to one another. If we stop it can go wrong, then we have stopped working together. OK, wait, stop, up a bit, let's take a break.

And in between, when there is room for it, when we have particularly good control, someone will crack a joke, and laughter comes easily to people when they are slightly tense, engaged in something requiring an effort. Agreements are made: if I do this, then you do that. We will bring it in this way first, turn it, and then it will go through. Now it is in place. Yes, good stuff!

It has been a good day. A mixture of pure toil, with the loading and unloading, and organization, getting everything in its proper place. We have worked hard. We can now tidy and clear up the last of the things and I can cover up and seal the hole in the roof. I have prepared everything beforehand so it will not take long. The cost of the day, including work done, crane hire, and supplies, is $18,000. The materials that have been brought up are like a blood transfusion to the loft. It has brighter days in store.

We unplug our tools, turn the lights off, and leave together, in our work clothes, for the pub.

19

JOHAN AND SNORRE ARE SITTING AT THE END OF THE bar at Teddy's. Beside them are two empty barstools. We quibble over who should sit down until eventually Ole and I take them. Dan fetches a nearby chair while Bård stands. It is not very crowded, but there are a few people around. The later it gets the more packed it will be, so we have arrived at the right time.

Johan and Snorre do not know the others that well but everyone is easy to get along with and they hit it off OK. We drink beer, enjoy ourselves, and after a while everyone gets a seat. The bar staff change, Engle and Kaare coming on for the evening shift.

We talk about music. Johan and Snorre are going to a gig at Gamla to see Harlan City Jamboree and Beat Tornados.

Beat Tornados are a good surf band; we agree on that. Dan and I would have liked to go but we are still in work clothes and are heading home after Teddy's. Harlan City Jamboree, on the other hand, I say, are shit, and that sets things off. Ole agrees with me and a lively discussion ensues. As Dan is trying to convince us otherwise, someone pokes me on the shoulder.

I have been standing at the edge of the group since coming back from having a cigarette a while ago, and I turn to see the guy who commented on Snorre's work attire a couple of months back, the one with the dress code at work. He recognizes us and asks if I too am a tradesman. It is really not that hard to figure out given what I am wearing.

He is having a pint after work again, but now he has something on his mind. It does not seem entirely by chance he came over for a chat. He says something about foreigners in the building trade and how inept they are. The irony in Snorre, a Dane, sitting right next to me is so obvious I do not bother pointing it out.

He tells me he has just had tradesmen in his house to do some renovation and redecoration. This is what he wants to talk about. There was no end of trouble and the place was a mess, he says; they never showed up when they were supposed to and so on. It is not exactly the first time someone in a pub has told me this.

"OK, OK," I say, interrupting him. "I'm not at work now and I don't actually work in consumer rights."

"I know, but all the same," he says. He does not let up, relates more details, gives more examples of just how stupid and useless these tradesmen were.

"So who were these people then? Where did you find them?"

"It was a Norwegian firm, had a Norwegian name in any case, and it was two Poles who came to do the job."

"And how did you find the firm?"

He had found them via an online service and through tips from people he knew. There were eight firms, and he had not even chosen the cheapest, he tells me.

"You don't think eight companies is a bit too many to ask to price a job?" I ask.

"No, they do it of their own free will; they come over and give a quotation."

He is right about that; they come of their own accord, nobody forces them, they are all adults.

"How cheap was it, if I may ask; what was the offer?"

"Forty-five hundred dollars, all aboveboard taxwise."

"And you checked their references?"

The ones he had picked came recommended by an acquaintance, and he had been given a list of references but had not bothered checking them. The job was not a big one.

"OK, how big was it in terms of hours, or days?"

"It took them a week."

"So you don't know the amount of hours involved. But two men for all of a week, can we say a hundred hours altogether?"

"Yeah, sounds about right."

I am tired and not in the best of humor now. I excuse myself and go to the restroom. While there I do a quick mental calculation from what he has told me. When I return he is still at the bar. He is talking to Snorre, about foreigners in the construction business, of all things.

"Y'know, what you're saying is quite interesting. Now I'll tell you what I think," I say. "I mean, if you want to hear it, that is. I'll give you my honest opinion but you have to be able to take it."

"No problem, I can handle an honest opinion," he says.

He cannot back out now, cannot be made to look like a wimp in the bar. He was the one who started it, after all, and he did say he could handle it, so I can push him that bit further. I am not quite finished doing the arithmetic, but have made a start and am pretty good at doing sums in my head. I also have pen and paper at my disposal now and place them on the bar.

"All right. So. You asked eight people out to your place to cost a job worth thirty-three hundred dollars excluding VAT. Once materials are bought in, that leaves them with around twenty-seven hundred dollars' wages for one hundred hours' pure work, as well as the six hours spent on inspecting the site and calculating the tender bid.

"You have been nice enough to invite eight different companies to work out a tender bid, so that makes it an eight to one chance of them landing it, which in turn would mean if everyone does that they would need, on average, to put together bids for eight jobs in order to get one. They need to cover the time spent on that, which comes to forty-eight hours. Are you with me?"

He nods. I continue.

"One hundred hours for the work and forty-eight hours of prospective site visits.

"The boss will want to get paid for the site visits, follow-up work, and other expenses. Let's say he's a modest sort and takes twenty-five dollars per hour for fifty-five hours of his own work, and a little extra to cover tool costs, vehicle, and everything else. That soon adds up to eighteen hundred dollars."

I ask him if he thinks the boss seems improbably well paid in this calculation. He does not.

"So, that leaves nine hundred dollars over for the inept characters that came over to your place to paint. That makes for an hourly rate of nine dollars, including holiday pay."

I speak calmly throughout, without the need to pause to think. Only stopping briefly to do a few simple sums on the piece of paper, it no doubt appears well rehearsed, but no matter.

"Nine dollars an hour, probably a lot of money in Poland, right?" I enquire, without waiting for an answer.

"And cheap here, cheap is the appropriate word, isn't it?"

He is quiet now, but I can see he is annoyed.

"I was just telling you about it is all, no need for you to be pissed off," he says.

"No, I have no need to be."

I have not behaved as if I am annoyed. I might have been difficult, but that depends on who you ask, and I am not quite finished.

"But you are a part of the big, greedy chorus telling the same smug stories. As soon as the opportunity arises you engage in social dumping, allowing you to be able to afford to come to this bar where I'm sitting and tell me yet another story about just how incompetent Polish tradesmen are.

"As well as which you tell it in an implicit tone to make clear that you do not think I am like them, I am better, which is supposed to make me feel happy?

"Listen, I guess it's true what they say, you get what you pay for. You only have yourself to thank for any problems you have had with tradesmen. If you're annoyed with me then that's just fine. We were sitting at the bar and you did approach me, so in a way you asked for it."

The conversation is over; we are less agreed than we were when it started. He is probably surprised by that, but I am not.

He is the same as the next guy. It has become common practice to use tradesmen, cleaners, or people who wash cars in this way. The customers are ordinary people, like the bloke in the bar; it does not matter to me who they are. I am more concerned with the ones doing the job. It could be me.

Dan heads home and Johan and Snorre go to Gamla. I stay for one more pint with Ole and Bård before trudging homeward along Grønlandsleiret.

The rest of the weekend is quiet, a bit of accounting, rest, and a stroll along the fjord from Bjørvika to Vippetangen.

20

ON MONDAY MORNING I KNOCK ON THE PETERSENS'
door and am admitted to a household in the middle of the
rush to work and school. It is a good idea to greet them at
the start of the week so they can see I am back at it after
the weekend. Kari and Jon have had a look upstairs since Friday
and are surprised at the sheer volume of materials we have
lifted in. I had been talking to them about maximizing the
space available in the loft and now they can see why. Jens and
Fredrik are curious and peek at me with interest, without
saying anything. They get their shoes and winter clothes on
and we each go our separate ways.

I want light in the loft, windows. It will make it easier and
more pleasant to work once they are installed. Winter is dark
enough as it is and daylight is precious. I start off by measuring
and marking up where they are to go. The windows are to be
located directly over those on the floor below; the planning
authority is very particular about that. Up until the late 1990s
many extensions and renovations on these types of apartment
buildings featured windows, dormers, and roof terraces located
at random around the roof, all according to the location of
the rafters, with no thought given to the facade. The powers
that be wanted to put a stop to that and introduced stricter

measures to ensure placement of windows was in accordance with the drawings and not the arbitrary nature of support structures. In many cases windows that had been built, even dormers, had to be torn out and reinstalled in the correct place.

With this loft I am lucky. There is only one rafter in the way of the windows that requires moving. With so much to be done on the roof, it is not much extra work anyway.

I begin by cutting away what needs to go from the existing roof construction in order to make room for the new parts that I will make. The roof must not be weakened too much, so step by step I cut the purlins supported by the rafters to make room for the windows. New rafters, at the edges of where the new windows will be located, serve as reinforcement. The roof boards, or wooden sheathing, I leave in place so the roof remains sealed and intact.

The windows arrive from Thaugland, and on Tuesday night Dan helps me to carry them up. He still has enough of his own jobs to be getting on with but comes to help out when necessary. We will make the holes in the roof boarding and put the windows in place tomorrow. Installing roof windows involves removing the sash, with the glass, and setting in the frame alone. Sashes and windowpanes are heavy and while it is possible to lift them into the frame on your own, it is no fun; it is better with two men.

On Wednesday morning I drive out to pick up a few odds and ends at Motek. They have a special offer on a cordless drill I am thinking of buying, as well as some construction screws that may prove useful, so I take the van instead of having them delivered to Hegermanns gate. In the end I decide against buying the drill; the one I have will do for the time being.

The radio is always on; in the van as well as on the building sites. The job would be a lonely one otherwise. On the sites where I am in charge there is an almost total ban on commercial radio. I cannot stand the excitable way everything is presented. Their delivery makes everything sound like one big, long adjective. My insistence on this has led to arguments with other tradesmen. Now and then I do have to give in, but not without a fight. A day listening to a private station like P4 is tiresome. So I listen to public stations, like NRK P1. In the mornings the latest on the traffic, news headlines, and weather forecast are the most important things on. It is snowing today; the wind is up and it is pretty cold. We will certainly notice it when we are standing in the openings for the windows, 50 feet above the ground installing the frames. The wind and snow will be blowing straight at us.

On P1 they are talking about weather conditions making people's travel times longer; there have been some minor collisions while a more serious accident on the E6 by Kløfta has meant the closure of one lane in a southerly direction. After the usual warnings about exercising caution while driving, about showing consideration, delivered almost like a devotional for motorists, comes a fresh weather update.

What are they actually on about in that breezy, morning tone when they talk about the weather? Apart from traffic and delays on the roads, the weather report almost entirely relates to leisure time. Except for the shipping forecast and its notices about the fishing banks at 5:45 a.m., weather and work are rarely mentioned together. Only at certain times, in the case of flooding or extreme drought, but it is still a far cry from the weather reports in times past, when the impact of the weather on work was important. The fisherman out at sea, the farmer, and the carpenter, those of us who do not choose when to be outside in the elements, we are no longer part of the conversation when it comes to weather. Weather is something that exists in relation to outdoor recreation, and is defined according to the depth of the snow and condition of the ski trails, or the sun and bathing temperatures.

The morning devotional is not far removed from commercial radio, just with calm, soft voices instead of the overexcited optimism of P4, so I change channels when it begins. It is odd how soft voices can also seem overwrought.

After zapping back and forth between different programs and channels I usually end up listening to NRK, the state broadcaster. When I am very concentrated on my work, I am not listening to what is on and forget to change the channel. I can understand how the segments in Sami might be a bit much for the majority of the people I work with. Personally, I think it makes for a pleasant change, the language floating in the background without my understanding a thing, merely voices and words without meaning.

Tower of Abel on P2 is a blast. I can carry out demolition work with a crowbar while they discuss why coffee sloshes about more in a cup than beer does in a glass. It has something to do with the froth, if I remember correctly, and the bubbles in the beer. Science lessons on the radio while I practice physics; I learn while working.

In the afternoons I usually listen to *Mrs. Larsen* on P13. It amazes me that the presenter, Kari Slaatsveien, manages to turn out such good radio year after year. I sometimes have to stop working to listen more closely and have done since she cohosted *Irma 1000* back in the early 1990s. I should maybe invoice her someday, for unforeseen loss of earnings.

Installing the windows does not take too long now that we

have done all the preparatory work, and we manage to get in four since we work a little late. I spend the next couple of days fitting the roof flashings on the outside and cutting the roof slates. The job can be carried out standing on a ladder in the opening but I wear a harness and am well secured inside. It is cold and dry so I do not need to worry about leaks.

Next week the winter sun can shine into the attic. Spring and warmth are a long way off but with the sun beginning to come up between 8:00 and 9:00 a.m. it is getting closer.

21

"MORNING, ALL." IT IS MONDAY, A NEW WEEK, AND I
greet the Petersens.

They are uncertain about how they want the bathroom
ceiling and I have brought along a few samples of tongue-and-
groove planks in aspen for them to look at. They have plenty
of time to make up their minds, right up until the last load of
materials is lifted up by crane.

There will be a lot of work with heavy materials this week,
up and down the step ladder and on the scaffold. It is enjoyable,
but also intense and arduous.

Normal timber comes in lengths of up to 17 feet, but
the rafters are almost 20 feet long. I have ordered extra long
2×9s so that they do not have to be spliced. They weigh around
65 pounds each and are unwieldy when precision placement is
called for. I make a "third hand" so I can work alone.

A third hand is a piece of equipment, knocked up from wood,
used to support and hold whatever it is you are assembling. It
is like having extra help and is one of my favorite terms in
my occupation. Making a third hand is almost like making a
friend, like James Stewart's Harvey. With the aid of a good
third hand I get the long rafters in place without any problems.

I use a laser measure to establish the length the triple 2×9s need to fit. I then cut a plank and lift it into place, before doing the same with the other plank that is to act as a rafter on the other side. The rafters cross one another at the top and when bolted together form a truss. I check how these fit, measuring for imprecision. I have marked copies of the lengths of these first two on another 2×9 in the stack, and adjust it according to the imprecisions I found. The next rafter will be a more accurate fit.

The tighter the truss connections, the more strength and stability is afforded the construction, as well as which it is easier and quicker to work this way. I avoid having to raise heavy materials up only to take them back down to adjust the fit, and I can stand on the floor measuring and cutting materials in comfort and safety. The weight of a 2×9 varies a lot depending on the density of the timber. One length can be almost twice the weight of another. I choose two light lengths for the first rafters in case I have to struggle with them.

All the 2×9s to be put together are glued and nailed. I put a suitable amount of glue on one surface and screw the two parts tightly together, before driving in 3.5-inch nails from a nail gun. It is a little like making laminated wood.

I repeat this procedure on the original rafters that the 2×9s will serve to reinforce, the result being a solid roof built upon the calculations the engineer has provided me.

I have made a roof truss. Roof manufacturers in Norway apply this as a catchall term for a variety of structures. They have taken a term that sounds good and used it for their products even though it often actually means something other than what they make. The term is an example of terminology in the field developing, and is now so ingrained that it is accepted as a technical term.

I get up a little later than usual on Thursday morning and spend the day on office work. I want to keep up to date with paperwork and have a tendency to shy away from it. The administrative part of running a firm is inevitable but it does not necessarily help move things forward on the site. I may as well have emptied a sack of peas out on the floor and then picked them up one by one, only to do the same thing over again. At least that is what office work often feels like.

This clerical work requires no physical effort, so it is in effect a rest day, and I try to fit it in at times when my back is particularly sore. In this way I try to make office work into a break when the body needs it. It is better than doing it with a gun to your head on a Saturday.

When I get up to the loft on Friday morning, the day spent shuffling papers has whetted my appetite to return to building. I get busy with the rafters and the follow-up fastening of the support structure.

Down at the knee wall I fix a 2×9 to the brickwork, bolting it tightly beneath one end, the feet, of the rafters. I fasten a mounting on each side of the rafters, attaching them to two 2×9s, which support them. Now the feet of the rafters are not going anywhere.

It is 8:00 p.m.; I am tired. The goal this week was to finish off the roof truss and I managed that. Now the new beam that will run beneath, supporting it, is ready to be fitted.

Goals like this are like little extra bright spots in the working day, giving me the opportunity to sit down, take in the work I have done, and experience a sense of satisfaction. They form conclusions but also the beginnings of what will happen next. Sitting looking around at what I have done makes me feel good, while at the same time I wonder if I could have done it differently, done it better. It is like a little building meeting in my head. I sit on the stack of materials and relax, consider how I will tackle the next stage, in particular how to fit the beam into place.

Time to go home and get a good night's sleep.

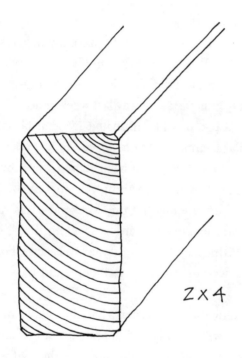

2 x 4

22

A QUIET, RELAXING WEEKEND. "MORNING, MORNING." We all greet each other on Monday and I make my way upstairs and drink a cup of coffee. I am relaxed and looking forward to getting started, but first caffeine, a look over things, and a think. This week begins the same way last week ended.

A 20-foot-long, 400-pound, laminated wooden beam lies on top of the collar beams. It is to be placed 13 feet above the floor, beneath the roof rafters. It has been stalking my thoughts the entire weekend. Having something like that at the back of your mind can be tiresome, but this weekend I was raring to get back to work, looking forward to tackling that, and to Dan coming on Wednesday. Working alone can become boring, so with two of us we not only get more done, but have more fun doing it.

For the time being the beam is just a big, unwieldy length of laminated wood. It will become an integral part of the support structure. Should someone remove it someday, the roof would not bear its own weight, or withstand the added weight of snow and the effects of wind. It would sag, or simply collapse.

The beam will support eight rafters on one side of the roof, running at a right angle to them, at a distance of 3 feet from the ridge. In order to stabilize it and provide maximum support to the rafters, I make a 4-inch notch, or bird's beak cut, into the rafters where the beam is to fit.

The roof is uneven across the entire way, so all the notches have to be made in slightly different places.

I use a chalk line in order to place all the cuts in a straight line running parallel to the ridge. I use a laser measure to ensure these cuts are level. This involves a fair bit of up and down on the ladder and on the traveling scaffold I have set up.

Twenty years ago, I would have messed around a lot before managing to get it finally right, but it is now a simple task as long as I carry it out step by step. Every stage makes the next one easier.

The "law of the lever" is a good friend to have when the beam is to be raised, as is the third hand. I use a combination of the two, letting them work together.

On either side of the beam I place two lengths of 2×4 standing on end with several 2×8s resting between them. It resembles a ladder with few rungs. I support this by fastening it to the collar beams so it cannot topple over. I make another such "ladder" and place them both at a suitable distance from the center of the beam. These ladders are a variation of the helping hand. The distance between them means the weight of the beam at one end is offset by the weight at the other. I can now use the law of the lever to seesaw the beam upward. I first lift one end and screw a transverse 2×8 tight underneath it, on the ladder nearest that end. Then I do the same at the other end. Up a bit here and up a bit there, without expending much energy. The distance between the ladders is exactly right to allow the balance of the beam to ease the lift, while the beam remains good and stable.

This makes it a safe method of raising the beam and saves

me the heavy lifting. In addition, it gives me the opportunity to move the beam sideways on the rig, adjusting the notches in the rafters should it prove necessary.

But I am not going to lift it now, not on my own. As of tomorrow we are two, and everything is lined up and in position for Dan.

It is early evening. The Petersens are home. I pop my head in and say hello before heading off. The whole family are together and have just eaten dinner. I notice my own hunger, but will soon be eating Indian food so have no reason to feel sorry for myself.

They look happy, the building is under way, and it is a big event for the family. I tell them the work is going according to plan, that Dan is coming tomorrow and then the pace will pick up.

Jon has been in touch with Get, the television people, and finally managed to have them fix a date to come and look at the cables. The telephone cables have already been taken care of. Get are coming on Monday.

"Would you like to take a look upstairs?" I say.

"Yes," Jon says, "we'd love to."

"I can show you what I've been up to and explain a few things. But you'll have to come up now 'cause I'm off home in a minute."

Jon and Kari start putting their shoes on but the children do not react.

"Don't all of you want to come and take a look?" I say.

"It's a bit dusty and dangerous up there at the moment," Jon explains.

The boys have obviously been given strict orders to keep away from the loft; that it is off-limits for a while.

"It's fine, as long they're careful. Would you not like to see, boys, if Mom and Dad don't mind, that is?"

Jon looks at Kari, who in turn looks at the boys, both of whom first eye me and then their parents. I have stuck my nose a little way into family matters but maintain a broad, innocent smile.

"Well, I guess it's OK," Kari says, "presuming the two of you want to?"

Jens and Fredrik leap from their seats and run toward the door, shouting in unison, "Yes!"

"You have to put your shoes on," she calls out.

"And you'll need coats, Mom and Dad too. It's cold up there," I add.

Before going into the attic I tell the boys they must not run around and to only go where I say it is OK to go. This also applies for the adults, but I do not say that. It is my ship at the moment, and given how untidy a site appears at this stage of the building work, it is like a ship in a storm.

I open the door and put the main plug in so all the lights come on at once. It makes an impression, especially on the children. From complete darkness to light everywhere. Their parents have not been up either since the windows were installed. They have probably consciously maintained a respectful distance, which is good in a lot of ways. Sometimes it is nice to be left in peace to get on with things.

They take in the windows, roof beams, all the materials, and the structure I have rigged up to raise the beam into place. There are no floorboards, only floor joists and clay. Visually it is a mixture of ruins and rigid structure. The roof frame and rafters cast shadows in all directions. The old materials are dark with age while the newer ones are almost white. It appears dirty and it is dusty. I do not consider dust as dirt. Dust is dust. I can become dusty, to the point of being completely gray, and then I can become dirty. They are two different states.

It smells dusty and is cold. It is hard to think of the loft as part of the home.

"That is where the bedroom is going. I guess the two of you will probably sleep there, will you?" I ask the boys.

"Where?" Jens asks.

I point, but it cannot be easy for a three-year-old boy to understand that what I am pointing at can become a room, with toys, beds, and everything that goes with it. His brother, on the other hand, is five and a half and willing to explain.

"He means there, over there."

Fredrik has understood.

"Our beds can go there, by the window. We can sleep under it."

Attic windows are new to him, so that is where he wants his bed. It is logical in a way, having your bed where you can look out, at the sky. Kari sees where he is pointing and explains.

"The ceiling is slanting there and is too low, so the bunk bed won't fit. Maybe you can have it over there, where the corner of your room will be? Wouldn't that be nice?"

It is a sweet moment. Kari and Jon can see the boys are excited, that they are starting to think of the loft as their own. Seeing the building site with their own eyes is quite different for them from listening to the grown-ups talk about it.

Jens and Fredrik eye my tools, the crosscut saw on its stand, the hammer and steel square in a pile with other hardware. Fredrik cannot help himself and places his hand carefully on the hammer, which is lying right beside him. He does not take hold of it, merely touches it as though it were something delicate, or dangerous.

"No! Don't touch that!" Jon says, stopping him.

"That's all right, there's no danger," I say. "You can pick it up; it can handle that."

"OK, if the carpenter says it's OK. But you have to ask first."

Fredrik asks politely and I tell him it is quite all right.

Children are often in the way when adults are going to carry out practical tasks. The adults then come to an arrangement where one of them looks after the children, gets them out of the way, while the other works, since that is more effective.

"When I'm going to hammer this nail, fix this shelf, you'll need to get the kids out, take them for a walk in the park."

Practical things become dangerous and the workplace becomes something akin to a potential crime scene where children can hold up the adult's work with their curiosity and nagging presence.

"Phew. It's heavy," Fredrik says, lifting the hammer with both hands. He cannot restrain himself and taps the hammer cautiously against the 2x9 it was laying upon.

There is a lot to look at and for me to show them, so I tell them they can try their hand at a little carpentry in a while. I point farther in and explain where the bathroom is going to be. We walk toward it, the boys almost reverentially silent.

"The bathtub will go here. That'll be nice, won't it?" I ask. "Do you like taking baths?"

Fredrik says that Jens is afraid of getting soap in his eyes, but that he himself likes having baths.

"Maybe it will be better with your own bathtub," I suggest to Jens.

He nods but does not seem altogether convinced.

"And that's where the toilet is going, there by the wall."

They struggle to picture how everything will be. The bathroom is harder for them to envisage than the bedroom, with everything that needs to be installed, all the plumbing and fittings. A bedroom is easier, just walls, a ceiling, and their own things. In a bathroom the decor is definitive.

They comment upon the bathroom, in their respective grown-up and childish manners, and then the viewing is finished.

"Right, it's getting late. I need to be getting off," I say.

"But you can take another look when I've done some more work. If you want to, that is?" I ask, aiming it mostly at the boys. And they say they do.

An Indian takeaway from Punjab Sweet House and a quiet evening at home. It will be nice to have some company on the remainder of the job, now that Dan will be working alongside me from tomorrow.

23

WE HAVE A THERMOS OF COFFEE WITH US. BOTH DAN and I prefer to bring one along rather than use a client's coffee machine, even though as a rule we are allowed to. It is cozy with a Thermos on-site, a little like being on a hike, minus the campfire, and with a lot more dust.

We sit with our cups looking at the drawings and at the attic. The beam is the first order of business, a carrot for us, the sort of work we look forward to. We will enjoy ourselves today; take things relatively easy. What is most important is that we get properly under way, together.

We have both done a lot of strenuous work lately. I am physically aware there has been a lot of heavy lifting, and the cold in the loft does not help. I have a few aches and pains, especially first thing in the morning. My body is tenderized, as it were, although it does not smart in one particular place but rather all over. Once I get warmed up things will get easier.

I lift the beam at one end, Dan stands ready with the 2×8, and we set to work. The law of the lever. Force times distance. Gears, pulleys, cogs, crowbars, all these operate on the basis of this principle of physics. It is my favorite law. I do not know what kind of food the people who built Stonehenge ate, or what language they spoke, but they were almost certainly fond of the law of the lever.

The beam is 21 feet long. There are two props for it, with a distance of about 6.5 feet between them, meaning we have to lift approximately 65 pounds, and even a guy who is stiff and sore like me can manage that. Using this method we could lift a beam the weight of a car if need be.

When the beam is almost in place we perform the last raise with crowbars. I know it will fit; I have confidence in my measurements and the notches I have sawn. Still, I do feel a little nervous excitement. We jack it up with the crowbars, place blocks between the beam and the props, and it slots into the grooves.

"That went OK," Dan says. "You were lucky this time!"

Just like my old boss used to say when we had done the thorough groundwork on a job. We secure the beam tightly with construction screws in the bird's beak cuts on all the rafters. The roof is holding up the beam for the time being.

We fit a post, a 4×4-inch-thick wooden pillar, located at the corner of the stairwell, beneath one end of the beam. It rests securely there. At the other end it is sitting in a cavity we made in the brick wall. Having already made a stable recess for it, we now place steel plates under the beam to bring it to the proper height. We fill in the cavity remaining around it with finishing mortar. The beam is now supporting the roof.

It is not hard to see how much better the result is with the beam positioned to the side of the ridge. We survey the roof with satisfaction, then dismantle the rigging, blow the tools clean, tidy up, and vacuum. We want it spotless now, or as spotless as a dusty loft crammed full of things can be. With two of us here it needs to be much tidier than when I am working alone. Working in your own mess is one thing, but working in someone else's seems much more chaotic.

A tidy site is a safer and more efficient space to work in, and it is nicer to come to work when the place is tidy.

24

DAN COMES BY TRAM THE NEXT MORNING. HE LIVES at the top of Storo, in Disen, and is happy to leave the car at home. Although it is not far for me to go, I still drive. Public transport links between Tøyen and Hegermanns gate are not great. It is also good to have the van handy when we are working, but the hassle with parking is frustrating.

Snow clearing in Oslo, in periods of snow like now in the middle of February, is mainly about moving snow from one place to the other. The roads are plowed and the sidewalks cleared, but the snow is only pushed to the sides in large banks, prior to motorists shoveling it back out onto the road again to get their cars out. After a few rounds of this kneading process, the snow becomes hard and heavy. To get the van out in the mornings I have to clear the snow from around it and when I get to Hegermanns gate I need to shovel snow away before I park. I repeat the same procedure in the evening when heading home, only in reverse, because in the intervening time the streets have usually been plowed again.

I have learned to clear the snow from around the van in the evening. It leaves less to do in the morning, when the snow is icy and harder. Any fresh snow that may have fallen during the night is easier to shovel.

The loft is cold, but we are used to it and dress appropriately. The winter has aggravated my eczema again; extra layers of clothing are no hindrance. The skin on my hands cracks and neither creams nor gloves help prevent it. I use surgical tape on the largest cracks; otherwise dirt and splinters can get in, and when the cracks are big enough they can begin to bleed. If we get sores, or cut ourselves, we use this tape. A small cut on the fingertip bleeds a lot. Surgical tape is the only thing that stays on while we work; bandages are no use, and the tape can be tightened and layered until it stems a little blood. If we sustain an injury beyond what can be fixed with the tape, we have to go to the doctor to get it checked out, and possibly get stitches. The threshold for considering a cut as serious is probably higher for people involved in occupations where the risk of injury is greater. I do not like blood, cuts, or pain in general, but notice I am less bothered by it on the job than when I change out of my work clothes. It is as though it hurts less, and you just get on with it.

Once finished with the rough work around the structural support, we fix fasteners to hold everything tightly in place, and set in some construction screws where required. The materials in our way will gradually reduce until the next round of lifting with the crane. Then it will once again be crammed with materials that will get in the way, things to work around.

I have been looking forward to tearing out the struts, ties, and surplus bearing structures. We place the wood and materials removed in compact piles. With the removal of those components, the old roof rafters need to be reinforced where they meet the crown of the wall. We use strips of iron here to secure the rafters against any movement.

The loft is now open, airy, and easier to work in.

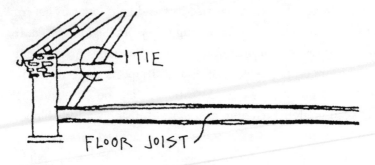

TIE

FLOOR JOIST

ORIGINAL CONSTRUCTION

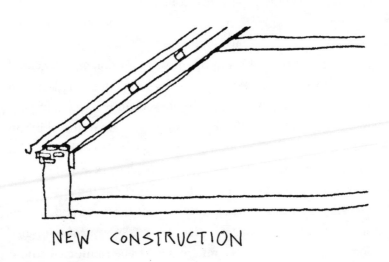

NEW CONSTRUCTION

25

THE WORK ON THE NEW STAIRWELL IS ONE OF THE tasks for which I think we have developed the best method. In perfecting it, we have made a lot of holes over the years.

The opening we are going to make will form the connection between an inhabited apartment and a dusty, noisy building site. Dust gets in wherever things are not properly sealed. Maintaining a divide between the loft and life in the apartment beneath is important and we solve it by not leaving the connection between the two worlds open during the building process. When we do open the hole completely, only a day of carpentry work will be required prior to the painter doing his thing, and the staircase can be installed. The customer experiences the minimum of inconvenience and that suits us too.

Down in the apartment we need to make a small opening in the ceiling in the center of where the stairs will go up to the attic. We use this opening to take the measurements we need in order to position the larger opening for the actual staircase.

Before we crane-lifted in the materials, I removed the clay from where the stairs are to go and put in some temporary sound insulation. We now remove that insulation and Dan goes down to the apartment. He takes a drill, a screw, a cardboard box, and ladder.

He drives the screw up through the ceiling approximately in the center of where we know the opening for the stairs will be. Taping the box tightly against the ceiling under the screw, he then stands on the ladder, supporting the box from below while I saw a hole about 8 by 8 inches from above using the screw coming through the floor as a midpoint. Since the hole I am making is in the middle of where the stairs are to go I do not need to be careful about the ceiling beneath and go at it with a reciprocating saw with a jagged blade.

I pick up the piece of roof I have cut out, then clean and vacuum around the hole and in the box Dan is still holding. When that is done, Dan removes the tape and the box and we have made a hole in the roof up to the attic without mucking up the apartment.

We place a point alignment laser on the floor of the apartment and point it through the hole up into the attic. This emits laser lights, along the horizontal and vertical axis, and is what is called self-leveling, so the laser gives us a precise reference point up in the attic and down in the apartment.

The new stairwell is to be positioned precisely in relation to two walls in the apartment. Using the laser, we measure the distance to one wall downstairs and then mark that off up in the loft. We then do the same with the other wall and mark that off up in the loft. We have now taken all the measurements we need from the floor below and can cover the hole again. Dan screws two layers of drywall tight to the ceiling, taping around the edges to keep out dust. That little hole will only be opened once more, when the man putting in the stairs comes to take height measurements. Then nothing until the opening is readied for the installation of the stairs at the very end of the project.

We eat at 1:00 p.m., a little later than usual. When I am on the job alone I do not observe any fixed times to eat. My stomach usually decides, and it generally lets me know between 11:00 a.m. and noon, but sometimes it can get to 1:00 p.m. or 2:00 p.m. before I notice I need to eat. Dan is more a creature of habit so we try to eat at 11:30 a.m. when working together.

While having lunch we try to refrain from shop talk, although it is difficult to avoid. It is good to shut out work for a while; your head is clearer afterward. We usually take our coffee in the loft but today we remain downstairs looking at the drawings and considering how to go about the rebuilding of the support structure. We have been given our own shelf in the refrigerator for our bag of food. Coffee from a Thermos flask is good but we are not that fond of packed lunches. It feels more like a real meal when we cut the bread and prepare the food there and then. The Petersens are taking care of washing our towels and do it more often than we would, so now we are living in the lap of luxury, both gastronomically and in terms of cleanliness.

One wall in the apartment carries on up into the attic. The finish on the wall upstairs differs from the one below, though, and we will have to take that lack of a layer of plaster into account.

Nevertheless, it is going in the same direction on both floors, meaning we can place our opening parallel to it. Therefore the measurements we took with the laser from below give us the placement of the opening, and the wall upstairs provides a direction.

The dimensions of the opening are 6×6.25 feet. We mark out a line parallel to the wall in the attic where one side of the opening is to be, and place a straight edge where our line is in order to have something simple to measure from.

In order to calculate an angle of 90 degrees we use the tradesman's simplified version of the Pythagorean theorem. If the three sides of a triangle measure 1, 1.5, and 2 inches, then the angle between the sides that are 1 and 1.5 inches will be 90 degrees, or a right angle. Using the same ratio we bump up the measurements to 40 × 60 × 80 inches, making a larger triangle and giving us a 90-degree angle at our straight edge.

We know where one of the two other sides in the opening is to be—it is where the other wall downstairs is—and we have marked that on a floor joist. We make our 90-degree angle here, and 6.25 feet from that we draw one parallel. Now the opening of our new stairwell is marked out. The wall forms the final side of the opening.

We then check the diagonals. If the diagonal lines within a square are equal then the angles of the corners must be 90 degrees. We must measure, check, and then recheck. We are working with precise dimensions on rough materials that are dusty and uneven.

I change the plug on one of the lights while we relax and wind down after the week. Better to fix it right away than let it annoy you for days.

Friday is an odd day. Most people, or the majority of them, are impatient for the weekend to start, and want the day to end. I often get a second wind at work on Friday afternoon. It is as though I can carry on free of obligation; the job is done, and everything I do is a bonus. I notice I want to stay, drag time out by talking, but Dan is having none of it; he wants to go home and I am going out to eat soup.

26

HELENE, SNORRE, AND CHRISTER HAVE WAITED UNTIL I arrive to order. Huế soup at Hai is the best-priced dinner alternative I know of in Oslo.

Helene works in a day care center looking after children; she is what is known as a "kindergarten aunt," and not having the right pedagogical education, she calls herself an "unqualified aunt." She is as sharp as a tack and fun to talk to, and together with Snorre and Christer, this makes for a pleasant little gathering.

When it comes to the prestige of the respective occupations of the people around our table, Christer is at the top, Snorre and I are in between, and Helene represents the bottom tier.

For a while the topic of conversation is quality of work. Has the difficulty of an occupation any bearing on its status, on how hard it is to deliver work of good quality? We are quick to reach a consensus, so our discussion soon turns slightly boring. There does not seem to be any marked correspondence between status and quality. Then Helene comes up with the bright idea of asking what quality is. Price, durability, functionality? Without doubt. Demand? Yes and no. The environment? Yes.

"No!" I say. "The environment, or what's termed sustainable production, is not part of the quality of a product."

"I'd definitely have to say it is; I don't buy things that are harmful to the environment. Well, not that harmful anyway," Christer says, "whether that's in their manufacture or in their use."

"Well, what about the flight you took to Barcelona last month then, and your mobile phone, with those rare metals? You like your smartphone; in fact you're addicted to it." Snorre's comments get the conversation moving.

"Yeah, but there're no real alternatives."

"Maybe no smartphone, no trip to Barcelona?" Helene responds, with not a little irony.

We agree to try and come up with a concrete example, a product we can discuss with regard to the raw materials used in producing it, the person involved in its manufacture, and its use. We land on a shirt.

"If the shirt is nice, well made, and I like it, then that's good enough for me," I say.

"So what you're saying is you only care about yourself!"

We order a fresh round of beers and Helene continues.

"In that case you can't whine about how people in your own line of work are treated. If your shirt is made from the worst materials from an environmental standpoint, and sewn by children in Bangladesh, then you have no business going on about the lot of all you poor tradesmen in Norway."

It is me against the rest.

"Listen, the fact the shirt is a good one doesn't mean child labor or destroying the environment is OK. Everyone buys what they want and has their own reasons for doing what they want, like Christer taking a flight to Barcelona and getting out his telephone to look at it every five minutes. I don't buy shirts sewn by children, not that I know of anyway. But that has little to do with the shirts the children sew. It is easy for us to say that they should have some kind of quality control based on children's living conditions in Bangladesh. We don't even have that here in our own country."

"We don't have child labor here though." Christer says.

"No, then again we don't sew many shirts here either—but that's not the point. We have our own laws prohibiting child labor. We also have our own laws to contribute to environmental sustainability. Shirts aren't sewn by children in our country because it's not allowed. So we can't rate the quality of shirts sewn by children here because there are none. The Working Environment Act and similar legislation are in a way superior to consumer rights.

"No matter how good the shirt from the child factory is all we can do is ban its import, on the same grounds we base our own laws. I suppose it's typical that in a discussion about quality we wind up relating our fundamental rights to a shirt. We would never justify the basic rights we have in our society with the quality of our clothes as a basis."

I have worked up a head of steam now.

"So you think we should use domestic labor laws, our Working Environment Act, for example, to assess everything we import?" Helene asks.

"Yes, to an extent. And then the problems with social dumping, in the craft industry here, will also be viewed as something serious we have to do something about. Or they ought to, because the problems should be easier to see in the right context. It is a significant and strange aspect of the times we're living in that the origin of things is borderless. We are all globalized people. Environment and working conditions are not limited by borders."

This is the kind of discussion that makes me happy to live in the society I do. Everything in the garden might not be rosy, but we do have options to prevent the total exploitation of people, and the complete depletion of our natural resources. It serves to make the disappointment all the greater when we, who live in relative luxury, fall short and make mistakes; after all, we are the ones who can afford to do right. Anyway, it does not take more than a drink or two to make me a law-and-order man and I propose a toast for the Working Environment Act. Everyone raises a glass to that.

"Without legislation to safeguard us we would have a completely different society than the one we have today. If we didn't have these protections then every parent would probably just have to pin their hopes on their children winding up on the right side of the factory gates. In other words, outside them and in school. Cheers!"

"I'm glad I didn't have to work with building things when I was thirteen years old; small children shouldn't have to sew men's shirts for a lazy elite," Snorre says, and we head off to Teddy's.

27

MONDAY MORNING. "HELLO, HELLO."

The family have been on a cabin trip over the weekend and have not seen the attic since the beam was put in place and the struts and ties were removed. They come up with me to take a quick look. The boys are wide awake, as children somehow can be without coffee, and tell me all about their cross-country skiing trips and sleighing. Dan is already up there, setting up lights and readying tools.

Kari and Jon like what they see. As planned, the beam does not obstruct the mezzanine in any way. The roof supports took up a lot of room. Even now, in the middle of the building process, with all the tools and stacks of materials, it is easy to see the space is a lot more open without them. It is coming along, as they say.

I have a few ideas for alternative solutions to the ones in the plans that, as yet, I have not mentioned. But now they have seen how we work and hopefully have faith in us being able to deliver what we have promised. They had planned on an Ikea bathroom but I suggest a fitted solution instead. It would be made from laminate countertop and cost a bit more than they have ordered. I show them a sketch, as well as a few photographs from similar jobs we have done for other clients. Kari and Jon are interested, so we agree I will e-mail them this material and they will think about it. I suggest the addition of an Ikea wardrobe on the mezzanine, adjusted to the sloping ceiling, so they get some Ikea too, and you can never have enough storage space.

It would be simplest to keep to the original job description and not further complicate the building process, but if they go along with my suggestions the bathroom will be a lot nicer and our job will be a lot more fun.

The Petersens leave and Dan pours us each a coffee.

A section of floor joists between the apartment and the attic needs to be removed for the new stairwell; what is left will require reinforcing, and we will have to redo the area of floor surrounding the opening. The new construction has been drawn and dimensioned by the engineer.

Instead of supporting the joists from the apartment beneath while carrying out the alterations, we secure them to the ceiling. This needs to be done while we are making the new construction to avoid the floor joists moving while weakened. If they do, it could lead to cracks in the ceiling below, and fixing that would be a major job.

We use 2×4s and a large amount of screws. These are reused later, as the assembled structure is provisional. Battery-powered drills and new and better screws offer us new possibilities in relation to this type of thing. The setup is simple and solid.

We spray polyurethane foam beneath the joists in the area where the opening will be. The foam fills holes and cracks, stiffens, and bonds everything together. It is one of the secret ingredients in our work and means we can make an opening for a staircase like this with a minimum of damage to the area in the apartment below.

flooring on top, giving us an unbroken floor space to work on. We insulate the hole, thus maintaining fire regulations—the loft remains its own cell where fire safety is concerned during the building period. The insulation also doubles as a sound muffler for the family below. We tidy up and remove the temporary setup that attached the floor to the roof. Now we can lay the flooring and make a start on what feels more like building a new loft.

28

THE PETERSENS HAVE ORDERED PRETREATED SOLID
pine flooring. This could be put down right on the battens,
but that would mean laying the floor now and covering it up.
Avoiding damage to the floor during the building process is
difficult, even with proper protection, so we will set down a
chipboard subfloor. The pine floor can go in later, when the loft
is all but finished.

The differences in height, or the slope, of old floors can be
considerable. An inch and a half in this case, so we are going to
even out the floor with new battens we can lay the chipboard
over. We spend the rest of the week leveling the floor.

On Friday morning Bjørn Olav, the electrician from Ebba's
firm, arrives to lay tubing with wiring under the floor. He
moves two old conduits to make room for the stairwell and lays
new ones to run beneath the chipboard subfloor. We write up
a plan for further electrical work, he makes a list of materials
he will need to bring next time and then he is off, the way
electricians are, onward to the next job.

Electricians are often here, there, and everywhere. It is a
way of working that would not have suited me. I like larger jobs
that keep me busy over a period of time. The trade industry
requires many different kinds of people, and one type are those

who like to always be on the go, doing lots of small jobs, zipping around in their own car. Bjørn Olav enjoys that sort of working day; he is his own boss in some ways.

Maintenance work gives me the opposite feeling: as though there is always someone telling me what to do. On larger jobs I feel like I am managing my time; there is more long-term planning, and several stages to the work. I perceive this as freer, while others see it as boring and stagnant.

The week has gone quickly. Steady progress; I am satisfied. It sometimes feels as though time is outpacing the work but I can see that this is going well, for the time being at least.

We finish off the last of the coffee and clock out. Dan is off to a child's birthday and is looking forward to some food. He is a chocolate cake kind of guy.

29

I POP MY HEAD IN AND SAY HELLO TO THE PETERSENS on Monday morning, and they tell me they have seen the prep work for the new stairwell. They were not in the attic much last week but went up on Sunday to take a look. I think they are trying to keep their distance from us while we work, simply out of consideration. They do not want to appear as though they are checking up on us but instead want to demonstrate their trust. It is a nice thought but unnecessary. I like it when clients keep up, are curious about what is happening. It can prove problematic when a client does not show confidence in us, queries the work, and puts things in ways that almost seem accusatory. Kari and Jon are not like that. Their manner of asking questions and the interest they display is fine. They are only too welcome to pop up to the attic more often; it is their home we are building, after all.

"It must have been a lot of work," Kari says, referring to the stairwell. "And no dust in the apartment; we didn't quite believe you when you said that."

"Yes, that should be all the dust you need to worry about from now until we're finished. Well, apart from us, coming down to eat and that. That's still OK, I hope?" I ask, slightly apologetically.

"No problem at all; you have to eat."

"Just ask if there's anything you're wondering about," I say. "Don't hesitate if there is something you're uncertain of. It can end up in misunderstanding and become a right mess. Just let me know if there is anything at all, and come up and take a gander now and again so you can see what we're up to."

Making use of moments like this to establish a relationship can be worthwhile, because if difficulties arise later on it might be too late. Then arguments and conflict can flare up more easily.

We are preparing to start on the floor and are ready to install the subfloor as part of that, so we chat a little about the flooring they have chosen. Solid wood feels softer than parquet, and looks better as well. The manufacturing process around it is friendlier to the environment, and that has also played into their thinking. Dan and I agree and tell them we like having the opportunity to lay a good, solid pine floor. All too often we put down parquet.

Parquet is slightly more reasonable, as it is faster to put down and that is probably why most people choose it, but there are several other reasons for its dominance. The large manufacturers, home decor, and DIY chains market parquet and laminate flooring heavily. It has become a loss leader in much the same way as pork chops and diapers in supermarkets.

Parquet is harder, does not scrape or mark as easily, and many people just like its appearance. Taste does not lend itself to debate, but a solid wood floor usually lasts longer, as it can be sanded several times. Viewed this way it is more durable, but people's relationship to things that are long-lasting has changed, it has become easier to buy new, and a lot of people can afford to. Parquet has become more reasonable at the same time as people have become less forgiving of wear and tear. As well as which it is easier to lay, requiring less effort on the tradesman's part than the floor we are putting in for the Petersens, so it has become increasingly common and as a corollary there are fewer adequately skilled tradesmen who can lay the solid wood variant.

I use the words *expensive* and *reasonable*. The words *dear* and *cheap* are not good; they are too expressive of a personal experience of costs, and I only use them when there is something wrong with the price. A vinyl floor is often viewed as inferior compared to solid wood. Both can be dear, but in that case that means they are overpriced. If the solid wood floor came at a reasonable price then the price is, well, reasonable. If the supplier of the vinyl floor has an extreme markup then I would say that floor could be termed dear, even though it still costs less than the solid wood floor.

I like both types of floor. They are both reasonable solutions and viewing it like that makes me less prone to snobbery. Solid wood flooring is more expensive but that does not mean vinyl flooring is cheap. People with a lot of money sometimes feel the need to show it, and snobbery is a cheap way to distance yourself from the great unwashed—cheap if you are rich, that is. The products themselves should not be a part of this petty struggle for status. A man's home is his castle, goes the proverb, and you should not dirty the floor when you are a guest, be it solid wood or vinyl.

We put down the chipboard on the portion of floor we have leveled, as well as over the opening for the stairs. We cut the subfloor to the exact dimensions of where the hole will be and leave it lying there. When the hole is to be made all we need do is take up the chipboard. With the "floor" now covering the stairwell the attic really is its own little world.

We move the materials that are lying on the remainder of the floor still to be leveled to on top of the subfloor. It does not take as long to install the rest of it. Once we have got the ball rolling the job goes quicker; there is less thought required or divergence from routine.

"The job is dancing a jig in my head now," as my accordion-playing old boss used to say.

The subfloor is installed and Dan launches into a little line dance, but fortunately the performance does not last long, not long enough for me to get "Achy Breaky Heart" on the brain.

Cleaning up will be a lot easier now, and we will be more effective when carrying out any work at a height, as well as being safer, now we have a flat floor to work on.

30

TOO LOW A PRICE OFTEN MEANS A LACK OF COMPETENCE, shortcuts, or both. When it comes to craftsmanship it is as simple as that, and this has nothing to do with issues of social dumping and worker exploitation. That you can run the risk of a poor quality job even though you pay a reasonable price is a whole different story. In this case, it is not the price that is the cause of a lack in quality.

Fireproofing an attic takes time and you can save a lot by making short work of it, but if it is not fireproofed the result is worthless.

It is akin to buying a large, expensive car with the security of your family in mind, purchasing good child safety seats, and having poor tires or worn-out brakes.

The analogy can be stretched further. It is as though you did this knowingly, because although the car was expensive, it was cheap compared to the list price, far too cheap. You brag to anybody who will listen about the price you got it for, but you know something must be amiss. You do not get a Rolls-Royce in good condition for the price of a beat-up Honda.

So if the loft is in effect a firetrap, but cheap as long as it does not burn, what would you call that? *Reasonable* is certainly not the word that springs to mind.

We are going to construct a firewall. In addition, we will screw drywall up beneath a portion of ceiling on both sides of the firewall, and fireproof the mezzanine.

The existing brick walls, forming a division between the apartment and the rest of the loft, are approved as compartment walls. The measures we will take are to be carried out in the loft itself.

Before making a start on the wall, we put in a new fire door from the old stairwell into the loft. The apartment and the rest of the loft are divided into separate fire cells and each must have its own door.

Containing a fire within the loft, and the wall we are going to build, is based on what is called EI 60. In practice this means a fire could be blazing on one side of the wall for 60 minutes before smoke or flames penetrate.

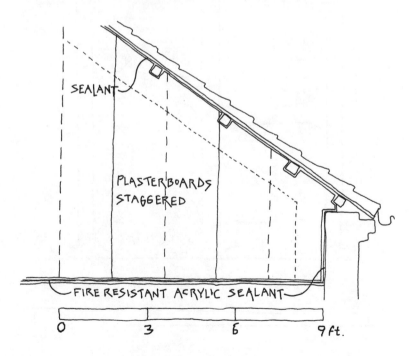

Firewalls can be built in many ways; the existing brick walls are an example of that. We are going to construct a double wall with a normal framework. The easiest way to explain it is to first describe a wall: 2×4 studs, with two layers of drywall on one side and the wall is insulated. The drywall needs to be staggered, that is to say there must be overlap to allow distance between the seams of one layer in relation to the other. The joints between the drywall sheet of the exterior layer are plastered.

The second wall is built the same way as the first and positioned at a little distance from it. These two walls are two sides of a firewall and also act as soundproofing.

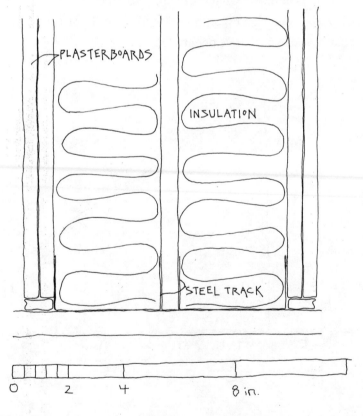

A gap of a quarter to half an inch is left between the drywall and the ceiling, walls, and floor, and this is sealed with fire-resistant acrylic. The sealant must have the correct width in relation to depth in order to function properly and prevent any smoke from seeping through. Placement of the drywall to obtain a proper gap is the most time-consuming part of building a firewall of this type, that is to say one under a pitched ceiling with purlins. It is also the part where people are most likely to do a shoddy job.

Smoke is the biggest killer in the event of a fire, which makes application of sealant a very important part of the work in fire prevention. The difference between a good and bad job in this case is a matter of millimeters.

31

I SLEEP IN AND ARRIVE AT WORK A LITTLE OUT OF breath. It is not the ideal way to start the week, so we sit down and talk about this and that before getting down to work. When stress first seeps in it has a tendency to pervade the entire working day, so a relaxing chat can be just the antidote to it taking hold. Dan has already been down to say good morning, so they know we are under way. The Petersens told him that they would like to take us up on our offer of a custom-built bathroom, and that they want aspen on the ceiling. The surfaces and benches will be in oak to contrast with this lighter wood above. They also want Ikea cupboards adjusted to fit the pitch of the ceiling on the mezzanine. These are nice jobs to look forward to.

We construct the framework for the walls and insulate them prior to putting the plasterboard in place. To make it easier, we lay the boards on top of two saw horses, making a desk of sorts.

We mark and cut the first plasterboard for one wall and make a reverse copy for the other side. The boards need to be perfectly perpendicular. It is important that we have a fixed form from which to measure the others.

Before hanging the first board we copy the dimensions of

half of it over onto a new board. This is for the second layer of plasterboard that will overlap the first, and extend 2 feet beyond the edge to avoid having a seam over a seam.

We then screw in the first board and its twin, its mirror image, on the other side.

We make the next section. Half of it is copied onto the half we have from before, which was copied from the first section we made. We then have another whole board to continue on.

Cut the board, copy, put in place, cut a new board. In so doing we cover both sides of the firewall simultaneously. This method means we measure less and copy more, which saves time, and also makes it easier to adjust the boards to avoid imprecision.

This game of duplication requires having an overview and working systematically but it yields good results when carried out properly. The methods we use are always open for debate. Which is best? You cannot measure the time it does not take, as my old boss used to say.

We apply the fire sealant with a pneumatic caulking gun. It applies a lot of sealant but the job is quickly done with the right tool, besides which we save our hands all that pumping. Where there are cables or wires passing through the wall we have to use a variety of sealants designed to expand at high temperatures and block the hole should the lead melt.

We fix a layer of drywall to the roof boards on both sides of the firewall and fill in the space to the wall with sealant. We are careful not to use long screws for the drywall on the ceiling. It would be an expensive mistake, because then we would have to lay new roofing felt. Up with the scaffold, off with the battens, counter battens, and roof slates to first get at it, then replace it, before putting everything back. The mere thought of a mistake of that size is painful.

The firewall is now finished and the loft is divided in two. The building site is one part, and when we refer to the loft that is what we are talking about. The rest of the area, where the storage rooms and drying loft are to be found, are outside. Just four months after Jon first got in touch the loft has become a place of its own.

We render the mezzanine fireproof, at the same time fix the battens, and put down the subfloor. Once that is done we have a new little dance floor, so I flash the lights but Dan deigns not to do a line dance this time.

Fredrik sticks his head around the door and he looks at us without saying anything.

"Well, hello! Is it time for a building inspection?" The door opens fully and the rest of the family are standing there. Or rather Jon is; Jens is safe in his father's arms.

"Yes, the boys wanted to come up and inspect; they're curious."

Jon places Jens on the floor. Dan invites them in.

"Come in, come in. Do you want to see what we've been up to?"

Jens nods, and pointing in the direction of the bedroom that does not exist yet, says: "We're going to sleep there."

"Do you see the wall we've built? You haven't seen that before, have you?"

Their bedroom is sectioned off from the rest of the loft, from the outside, now that the firewall is up. Fredrik walks over to it, looking like he thinks what is happening is strange. Their loft has a floor now as well.

The boys take a look around. Dan shows them how to draw

on the floor with bits of plaster; they are allowed to do that even though they get a bit dusty from it. We have a grown-up talk about how the build is coming along while the two building inspectors busy themselves with their plans.

Dan and I tell them it is going well and everything is on schedule. We discuss how they want the bathroom fitted out and the tongue-and-groove wood on the ceiling. They thought solutions like that cost too much and were not aware a carpenter could provide them. I say they cannot be sure we can yet, make it well enough that is. Then I assure him they will be satisfied. We know each other that bit better now and can joke around a little.

The building meeting is over. Dan and I tidy up a bit but leave the proper cleanup until Monday. We have done enough for one week and are satisfied with getting the firewall and mezzanine finished. Some clutter in the loft will not do any harm; nobody else has any reason to be up there before we come back after the weekend.

32

"GOOD MORNING." A NEW WEEK. BOTH FREDRIK AND Jon are suffering from colds and are staying home today.

The morning is spent tidying up the loft, removing debris, and catching up on outstanding bits and pieces.

We sometimes eat lunch at Café Bentse and it suits us today, seeing as how they are at home sick in Hegermanns gate. Dan wants roast pork and I order meatballs and stewed cabbage.

The old guys, the regulars, are in their usual seats discussing betting, politics, and all manner of things. Lian, who works here, provides the entertainment as usual, exchanging good-natured banter with all the guests. By the door a guy sits quietly minding his own business, and he is left undisturbed. Which is not to say he is forgotten; he is also well taken care of.

A couple of elderly women from the area enter and soon join in the old men's discussion. Lian flirts and teases them as though they were two young ladies on a night out. This is one of the nicest eateries I have come across in Oslo.

Food and coffee; we talk shop and a little about everyday life.

I have a good impression of Kari and Jon Petersen. They show initiative, get things done. Jon sorted out the cables in the loft, for instance, and when we agreed the contract and signed it was all very organized and proper. They want solutions and accept the decisions made. At least that is the impression I get.

"If they're wondering about something they ask genuine questions, which I like. They ask without making it seem as if they're trying to tell me how to do my job. And there's a pleasant atmosphere in their place, with the boys and how everyone interacts."

Dan agrees, nice people.

It is lovely working for clients who know what they want, have clear wishes, and are appreciative when things turn out as they wanted.

We discuss how to approach the rest of the job. I am keen to make a start on the bathroom floor, while Dan has a mind to take the ceiling next. It will mean using up a lot of the materials and he wants to get rid of what is still up there so we do not have to move them around unnecessarily. The advantage in taking the bathroom first is that there is a lot to be done in there and getting it under way would be good. It is always nice having plenty of time. In the end we decide there is enough time for the bathroom, even if we start on it later. My impatience was a reflex response, an unconscious twitch in the hurry muscle. Patience is one of the most important tools of the trade and the work on the loft is going well. It is odd how stress can crop up when you least expect it, even when there is no reason to get stressed-out. It is a good thing Dan keeps me in check, and slightly surprising, because usually it is the other way around.

The two of us can discuss the best way to do something, and being two makes it easier to remember everything we should.

We may disagree but there is no pride involved. The discussion always needs to reach a conclusion and a decision made, and we then carry out the solution picked even though one of us might disagree. This is my project so I have the last word. Dan wants it that way; on his projects it is the other way around. We work as a team but one of us has the responsibility of a boss.

Whenever I have cause to carry out practical work with academic types, the divergence in working practice is made clear to me. It seems as if they are trained in a culture of debate where the outcome, the conclusion, does not weigh as heavily.

Instructions on a building site are often fast and forthright, almost like orders. Those with an academic background can become irritated or angry when they are clearly told to do something or other. They can start a discussion in the middle of lifting something heavy and turn the heavy lifting into a study group.

Submitting to a decision, or to authority, is not the same as being subservient. Lifting something together is a good example of how, when the decision is made, the discussion is over; then we act in unison, no matter that we are not in agreement. Then the difference between talk and action is made clear. Perhaps academics would prefer if the instructions given were wrapped up in more diplomatic language but there is not always time for that. I often find them tiresome to work alongside, even though there are exceptions and they are a pleasure to encounter.

Dan and I agree to start on the knee walls and the roof. We reminisce a little about previous loft conversions we have done, to brush up on how we usually do it. Reminiscing is a mix of serious shoptalk and self-praise. We have faith, the way you might have when fishing, but are also critical of our own methods. Is there anything we can do better? On leaving Café Bentse we know how we are going to begin the work and have a reasonable idea how to tackle the job of the knee walls and the roof in their entirety. We have the same film rolling in both our heads.

Warm air retains more moisture than cold air; that is what you see when a mirror fogs up after a shower. The glass surface cools down the air and it releases some of the moisture. The air inside a heated house contains more moisture than cooler air outside. When the warm air inside moves outside via roofs and walls, it cools and needs to release moisture. We have to make sure that what happens with the mirror in the bathroom occurs in a controlled manner in the roof and walls.

This is fundamental in understanding how we build houses in Norway. Major mistakes will have major consequences, guaranteed. A house can rot to the core in the space of a few years if craftsmen do not pay attention.

Externally there has to be something to protect against the weather—roof slates, for example, or paneling on the outer walls. Behind this exterior there ought to be a layer of air to allow moisture and condensation to dissipate. Behind this a windproof material, and behind that again, insulation. Underneath all this, against the inner climate, is usually plastic sheeting. The materials used may vary but the principle remains the same.

Obviously there are aspects of a construction like this that could contribute to a poor interior climate, but if done correctly the indoor climate will be good. A lot of the time I have to explain to clients how all this is connected. Wearing the right clothes in bad weather is similar to how we think when building, an analogy that is often easier understood than explanations about thermodynamics. On this roof there are already new roof slates on battens and counter-battens, as well as the sheathing or membrane. This keeps it waterproof and impenetrable to wind, and is breathable, almost like a Gore-Tex jacket. The outermost layer of the roof is finished. Dan and I are going to lower the ceiling and insulate and plaster it.

33

IT IS EASIER TO BUILD STRAIGHT THAN CROOKED. IF YOU have a plumb bob, a spirit level, a try square, and straight lines, then you have dependable starting points. What is crooked is without control. Botching up and building something asymmetrical when it should be straight is actually quite eccentric because there is no logic to it.

Building the right way requires knowledge and skill, but that also makes it easier. The sight of poor finishing on surface work makes me skeptical about the quality of what is beneath, the work not visible to the eye. I start to wonder if the insulation and ventilation have been done properly, or if there are any possible dangers of leaks in the construction.

Most people would say the most common cause of poor building is carelessness and cutting corners, but I do not think so. The usual reasons are a lack of know-how, not having adequate time, and poor management. If you get a tradesman who is not proficient in his field to do a job, add in being pressed for time and a boss who does not follow up on the work, then the likelihood is it will go wrong. Throw in language difficulties and cut-rate prices and the chaos will be complete.

We establish straight starting points in the attic, beginnings we can work from. Good craftsmanship starts with the first chalk lines, with a level and laser and the 3:4:5 ratio in a right-angled triangle. The beginning is in many ways the most difficult because considerations are taken into account and decisions made.

In order to assess the work we have to think far ahead.

There are always inaccuracies; this is unavoidable. Experience is important in knowing when to spend extra time on precision and when to keep on going. The trust Dan and I have in one another and the differences between us in character are perhaps our most important tools as colleagues. We offset each other's good and bad sides, get the best out of two ways of thinking. What might be the right way of thinking at one moment may be wrong the next. Some of the best days I have had are those where we have intense discussions and I arrive home feeling we both contributed to getting a lot of good work done. At times like that I almost feel devoted to Dan, because he accepts me as I am while simultaneously managing to remain himself.

Mistakes are inevitable, but dispensing with tolerances is stupid and unnecessary. Imprecision is not necessarily a problem unless there is a lot of it. When the mistake from the valley meets the mistake from the village at the dance there will be trouble, my old boss used to say. He came from somewhere in between the two himself.

The most important thing experience teaches you is that you have deficiencies, holes in your knowledge. After all, it is not easy; you cannot know what you do not know, so how can you be alert to it? When do I need to stop and figure something out? Go on the Internet, ring fellow professionals, the architect, or the engineer?

Knowing your own limitations is the single most important attribute a good craftsman has.

This must be learned through practice. I can say it to an apprentice but at the end of the day it needs to be learned over time, through work.

Making mistakes is the best way to learn about what you do not know, what you are not capable of. Through mistakes you learn how important it is to understand what you are doing. A good firm in which to learn your trade is one that tolerates mistakes while at the same time supervising an apprentice's work to the extent that the mistakes do not become too large.

A good professional often has a peculiar mix of confidence and uncertainty. A sort of specialization created by a split personality, as though their confidence depends on their being uncertain. Their desire to avoid mistakes springs from an unceasing stream of questions. These questions are derived from experience and help a craftsman to fulfill his potential.

Someone building something crooked is either too sure of themselves or not unsure enough, my old boss used to say. He was like a block of granite in discussions and I only managed to knock off a few chips, at most. He was best when discussing with himself, but it took me a while to understand that he was stricter on himself than anyone else. And like a block of granite he was good to lean against.

34

THE FLOOR, NOW LEVEL, IS OUR STRAIGHT STARTING POINT. We will also use the center of the roof ridge. Placing the point laser on the floor under the middle of the ridge of the roof, we find the center of each end. Using a chalk line, we join up these two points, marking the position of the roof ridge out on the floor.

We then measure from this line on the floor to the knee wall, drawing a line parallel to the first one to mark where the knee wall will run. The other wall will be in the bathroom but we leave that for the time being.

The knee wall is a very particular part of this type of conversion. The attic is going from being airy and open to being closed off behind walls and ceiling. The knee wall is the meeting point between the masonry in the walls and the roof rafters and roof boards. It is a vulnerable spot for fungal growth and dry rot. Wood decay is bad enough but true dry rot is catastrophic. If you build incorrectly you are, in the worst case, constructing something comparable to a hothouse for micro-organisms, and the question is not whether damage will occur but when.

The wind- and damp-proofing of the wall need to be done carefully to avoid moisture penetration. In addition, airing must be adequate. Between the insulation and the brick wall I make an extra-wide air cavity, 4 inches instead of 2 inches. Getting fresh air into that cavity is simple. I hire people to core-drill holes in the brick wall. This is done from inside the loft, where it is OK to work. Done early in the building process, the resultant mess from the water used as coolant when drilling is easy to tackle.

These holes allow for good ventilation of the air space within. When the holes have been bored you need to fix grilles on the outside to cover them. This requires the use of a cherry picker but there is no rush, so we will carry out that work at a later date, when the snow has gone and we have rented one for other work to be done on the roof.

It hits me that there was no mention of airing of the knee walls in the project specifications. I knew of course that they are necessary but did not remember to check. It is a cost I expect the Petersens to bear. When I tell Jon about this he is not happy and I notice his reluctance when I describe the work that needs to be done and the cost. We need to reach a decision soon; he agrees with me on that much and says he will ring the architect right away.

Dan and I continue with what we are doing. We adapt the plan and construct the wall such that the wind layer can be opened to make holes in the wall and then sealed tightly afterward.

We are careful to insulate well down beneath the floor where it meets the masonry, to avoid a cold bridge, an area transferring cold air from outside in. The wall studs are set in a steel track on the floor and fixed tightly to the roof rafters above. The wall now provides a good basis to start on the roof.

At each end of the wall we measure 12 inches out from the

roof and mark it off on the studs. We now have the thickness of the ceiling and space for insulation. The ceiling is crooked so we adjust the two marks we have made to be level in relation to one another. Using the chalk line, we mark a line along the whole length of the wall across all the studs. It is here that the corner, or angle, between the ceiling and wall will come, and it is now completely straight and level.

We run a bendable steel strip along the line we have marked on the framework for the knee wall and now have a nailing strip for the "corner" where the ceiling and wall will meet. The steel band is perforated in the center and 4 inches wide, allowing us to bend it to the angle desired. We still use terms like "nailing strip" for the steel material even though it is intended for screws and drywall. The corners we build in this way are completely stable, with no fracturing between the drywall sheets.

The steel band is like a sill for the ceiling and is easily built upon.

The ceiling has a pitch of 36 degrees. The gable wall is as good a place to start as any. We fix a 2×4 to the wall using the steel band on the knee wall as a basis and use a torpedo level to find 36 degrees. On the firewall at the other end of the room we do the same. We attach a string held by nails at the top and bottom of each 2×4 at a distance of half an inch from their surface. We can now adjust the 2×4s along the strings until they are straight. The ceiling is now demarcated by steel at the bottom and 2×4s on the sides, so we can get straight down to it on Monday without too much fiddling about.

We finish up for the weekend and Dan goes home to his family while I stay on so the Petersens and I can have a little review of the work so far. Kari's father has come to take a look.

They bring coffee and Danish pastries up to the attic. It is my first time meeting him, but Kari has informed me that he has been up to take a look before. He has said our work looks good, and I am told that his putting it like that is quite the compliment. He now gets to see some photographs from the building process and stairwell construction and commends us on our method of avoiding dust and mess below while making the hole. We chat about how we will proceed and he asks about details like the membrane on the bathroom floor and walls, but mostly we talk about how it will be when it is all finished. I apologize to Kari and Jon for forgetting the ventilation holes in the knee wall, and they say that there is a lot to think about so it is understandable. Kari says there is a lot more involved in a conversion like this than she would have imagined, so it is not strange something might slip my mind. The bill for boring the holes should not be a problem.

Jens and Fredrik run around looking at tools and materials. They are allowed to borrow a hammer and a few other things. They draw on small pieces of wood, hammer away, and discuss what they are going to make.

"A boat," Jens says. He has found an offcut sawn at an angle at one end. When he puts a little block of wood on top for the wheelhouse it becomes understandable to us adults as well. Fredrik wields the hammer and with a nail and a little assistance from his grandfather the block is fitted in place. I tell them they are free to draw on the floor of where their room will be, and using a pencil, they sketch a type of bed out where they think it should go, as well as the rocking horse that will live there with them. The building meeting with the family comes to a close. They remain in the loft a little while longer while I head on home.

35

MY LAID-BACK WEEKEND CAME TO AN ABRUPT END
on Monday morning when I awoke half an hour after the alarm
had gone off. I need to stop sleeping in. Spring is tentatively
under way, but I am still feeling the aftereffects of a long winter.

I poke my head around the door and get the Monday morning greetings out of the way. The boys call out when I come
and will not let me leave before showing me their boat on the
living-room floor. A mast and sail have been added. Their
grandfather helped them. They tell me they are going to sail it
at the cottage in the spring.

"Maybe you can sail it in the bathtub in the new bathroom
too," I suggest.

They think that is a good idea and I head up to the attic
while the discussion on bathtubs and sailboats flows back and
forth in the apartment.

Dan and I continue on the ceiling. At the top, by the roof
ridge we arrange a provisional setup for the nailing strips,
which we straighten up with a string stretched tight along it
from end to end.

I am glad I ordered extra-long 2×4s that stretch from the
top to the bottom of the roof surface now. We can easily put
them in place and fix them at a spacing of 2 feet, from center to

center, up along the setup and 2 feet apart below on our steel sill. After we have straightened up the 2×4s with string all across the middle of the pitched ceiling surface and fixed them tightly to the setup hanging between the roof rafters, we have a dropped ceiling with minimal deviation.

We copy the line of the ridge we have marked on the floor to our nailing strips at the top, attach an angle corner along the line, and the nailing strips along the interior ridge in the ceiling are finished. We have now dropped one half of the ceiling. This new interior ridge will act as the starting point for the lowering of the other half of the ceiling.

We have spent years working out this method of dropping a ceiling and do not know anyone who does it quite the same way. The same goes for how we made the hole for the stairs and for pretty much everything we do, in a way. We have learned parts from other tradesmen, then Dan and I have developed these ideas further. There is no description of how these types of things, typical craftsmanship that is, are solved in practice, so the tradesman must find a solution himself. If I met somebody who had a better method I would be only too happy to adopt it.

I have my own experience. Learning from others is important but experience is personal to the extent that you could say it has become part of my personality. Instead of being reincarnated as something magnificent I would like to be reborn a tradesman many times in a row with my experience intact each time. A few reincarnations from now and I will have it down pat. But I want a new back every time.

The complexity of the work on the roof can be demonstrated by the number of tools involved. We use a torpedo level, a point laser, laser distance measure, tape measure, a folding ruler,

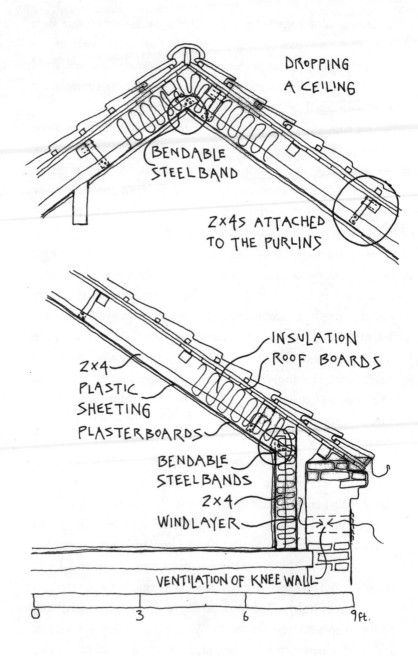

DROPPING
A CEILING

BENDABLE
STEEL BAND

2×4S ATTACHED
TO THE PURLINS

INSULATION
ROOF BOARDS

2×4
PLASTIC
SHEETING
PLASTERBOARDS

BENDABLE
STEELBANDS
2×4
WINDLAYER

VENTILATION OF KNEE WALL

0   3   6   9 ft.

try square, chalk line, string, a straight edge, and a pencil for measurements.

Measurement, calculation, and precision are easy to apply to life as metaphors. An excessive need for accuracy is not positive but neither is something being crooked out of sloppiness. Precision varies from trade to trade. Where metalworkers work in hundredths of millimeters and less, I work in millimeters and centimeters. Masons tend to deal in slightly larger tolerances than carpenters. The precision of the craftsman also depends on the situation. Different parts of the job require varying accuracy.

Good precision in craftsmanship is not dogma but necessity. I have met a few people in the course of my job who have had a bewildering attitude toward accuracy, almost viewing the need for it as an attack on their personal liberty. They often conceive of themselves as having a particularly well-developed sense of freedom. They "mix it all into a gravy," as we say in Norwegian, and think the custom of good craftsmanship is the same as submitting to authority, as kneeling to power. They want to be free to improvise, or as I see it, to do what they want. They will never make good craftsmen.

That gravy expression probably originated in the kitchen. It would be apt in any case, because if you mess about with the fundamentals of the craft in a professional kitchen it is going to go wrong. Cooking is a field where technical discipline is particularly pronounced. A lot of chefs seem a little crazy, but do not let that fool you; the best among them are tough professionals. Perhaps the difficulty of the occupation and the intense working environment, with strong demands on time and tempo, puts its mark on them, or else the occupation attracts those who are like that.

In order to deviate from what is exact in a craft you need to know what is right. Without this knowledge things become random, like in a lottery.

This blend of independence and recognition of professional authority and discipline is one of the best things about a craft.

36

THE STACK OF MATERIALS IS DIMINISHING AND THAT IS a good thing; they have become more than seemingly random objects—they are completed work. It is the end of March, and the loft is something quite different than when Jon Petersen rang me for the first time in November. The birds have begun singing tentatively outside. My eczema, coming and going all winter according to the temperature, has almost cleared up. Spring is on the way.

New materials are needed; we are beginning to run low. We do not have enough to lower the entire ceiling on the side where the bathroom is to be built, but we have enough to make the most important parts, the framework and parts of the knee wall.

We do as much of this work as we have the supplies for. Small nailing strips are to be fixed in many places and for these we use the offcuts, the short pieces we have left over from building the knee wall and lowering the ceiling. Waste is money squandered, and when left as rubbish needs to be transported away. If you work in a smart way there is less waste; that is foot after foot of money saved, and is one of the most direct contributions we can make in terms of resources and the environment. It could be a scene in a dream, a huge, smiling piggy bank, and me putting in bits of materials instead of coins. In keeping with the eco-friendly aspect of the dream, the pig could be free-range.

The plan for ventilation of the knee wall is approved and the Petersens will cover the cost. That is a relief. There was no debate or back-and-forth; Jon just sorted it out. He almost lets out an audible groan over the telephone when I tell him that I will need a written description of the solution, with the dimensions of the holes, their number and placement, in an e-mail from the architect. It is the way it works in the building trade—you have to cover your back. I have no choice but to pester him for it.

I have called up Jukka and asked if he can come and bore the ventilation holes, and he can make it on short notice. I actually rang him as soon as the problem first cropped up. He works for a large construction company, but I only deal directly with him. Having a good relationship with people in different firms is handy; things get sorted more easily. It can sometimes seem as though they are sympathetic to guys like us, in smaller firms, and do their bit to help us out.

Jukka produces his big Hilti machine and his day begins with the bit and barrel jamming and then breaking, so he needs to fetch a replacement and spends a large part of the morning in traffic. He does the job for me, but he has a long day in front of him since he has to get on and finish off another job as well. He swears a little in Finland Swedish for appearance's sake, but he is in good humor all the same. I make sure the windproof sheathing is sealed and ready the knee wall for insulating.

Thomas comes on Friday morning to do the plumbing. He is a nice guy, good at his job, and easy to work with. He is accident-prone, in his free time mostly, so it is not unusual for him to be wearing bandages after trying out some tool or other that he is not entirely familiar with. A power planer for instance; I can hardly bear to think about it, a plumber and an electric planer. They do not belong together. We have done the preparatory work with demolition and making holes for his pipes, so that Thomas can get right down to the plumbing.

He puts the drain for the shower and the outlet for the toilet in place.

All the main drains, the soil pipes, need to be ventilated. When you flush a toilet and the water runs down the drain there is suction on the water in the trap. Without the presence of water here the stench of the sewage would come up into the apartment. By airing the soil pipe you avoid this, and the ventilation is led above the roof, where the smell can blow away without bothering anybody. We will place covers over the pipes coming through the roof later. Thomas does what needs doing at this stage and then the bathroom is ready for Dan and me to get started on.

Building a bathroom requires a lot of work, incorporating a variety of tasks across a number of fields of expertise. We will all be involved: carpenter, plumber, electrician, mason, painter, and membrane specialist. Everyone will play a part and it all needs to be done in the right order. A new bathroom, like the one we are to build, costs in the region of $30,000. Well, actually more than that, due to the preliminary work carried out on floors, ceilings and walls, which form part of the overall loft conversion.

The madness that can ensue when people want a bathroom built is a frequent topic of tradesmen's conversations. If someone offered to build an equivalent bathroom for

$20,000, the chances of it turning out all right would be slim. Where would the other $10,000 be saved—in materials or in pay?

The membrane at a slope to the floor drain is firmly clamped with a ring; this is what makes a floor waterproof. Johannes told me a story about a new bathroom that he had to tear out and build again because the membrane was attached around the outside of the drain. This is more commonplace than you might think. In the Petersens' bathroom we lay drainpipes for the sink, the washing machine, and the shower drain on top of the membrane to insure them against leakage. The steel mesh for the cement is placed over the pipes, with the under-floor heating cables attached to this mesh so that they end up in the middle when the floor is poured, and the heat is distributed nicely.

The tiled surface is laid at a gradient so the water from the shower runs into its drain and the rest of the room slopes toward the main drain.

A new lift by crane on Friday; the materials have been ordered and once again Svenn will have his hands on the controls.

The volume of materials is larger than last time, because now all the insulation for the roof and walls is being put in. The insulation is placed up on the collar beams in the storage area and wherever else there is room. We take in wet-room panels, drywall, fasteners, adhesives, sealant, plastic sheeting, lots of odds and ends. Bathroom tiles and mortar for Johannes as well. Using the crane pays off.

The mortar for the floor weighs approximately 1.3 ton; that is more than fifty sacks of fifty-five pounds each. It would have meant fifty trips up the stairs to the loft, in addition to carrying up the tiles and the adhesive needed, which is about the same again.

This time we do not sort the waste; everything goes into one skip, being cheaper than two half-empty ones. Still the skip is not full, so the Petersens are allowed to top it off with some of their own junk. Jon has knocked off work early today to throw out what they want to get rid of. Bård gives him a hand with a sofa and some other larger items.

We now have plenty to keep us busy, lots of new supplies. With all the work we have done and the material replenishment, we have a good feeling of being on the right track. Everyone deserves a pat on the back.

Today we are going to eat cake. I drop by the bakery in Åsengata and buy cinnamon rolls and custard buns. Thomas puts in a special order for mille-feuille from Baker Hansen. It is not often so many of us are gathered, and it is Friday, so we decided to have a little get-together. Jon makes us coffee and we have a little tea party sitting on the stockpile of materials.

I close off the hole in the roof and another week is over, of work, that is. This will be my first weekend off in a while, not even any paperwork.

Ole joins me for a trip to Hurumlandet peninsula on Saturday to fish sea trout. The weather forecast promises sun and no wind, so we take the year's first *proper* trip, as we call it. We have both fished a little earlier in the year, but we envisage this trip as a beginning, a transition to the good spring fishing, and it imbues us with faith, not that the fish bite any harder for that reason. When angling it is important to believe, just like at work.

Ole always thinks the fishing is better at another spot than the one where he is standing, and often has to move, preferably somewhere harder to reach. This time he steps off a stone, miscalculates the depth, and plunges in, ending up in water up to his waist. It is the first time I have ever seen someone standing in waders filled with freezing cold water. The shock of the cold makes him gasp for air like a trout on land. We empty his boots and he gets the rest of the coffee, and I laugh the whole way back in the car. We may not have got a bite, but the trip was a success in terms of fishing stories.

37

I SAY HELLO TO THE FAMILY ON MONDAY MORNING and begin the week with a clear head from our fishing trip. I cycled to work for the first time this year. The ascent up the hills to Torshov was hard going, but it will get easier in time. The choice between bicycle and van will play a part in my planning from now until after the summer. Should I need the van in the course of the working day I will drive; otherwise I will bike it, unless of course I am too lazy.

Cycling gives me a sense of freedom, of not being dependent on the car or on public transport. Throwing my leg over the crossbar at the end of the day, I feel even more finished with work than when I get behind the wheel of the van.

The knee wall runs the length of the bathroom. The room is rectangular and approximately 110 square feet. At one end the bathtub will run along the gable wall, and at the other, the wall near the existing stairwell, the toilet and shower will go. A bench will be placed against the knee wall, where the washing machine and dryer will stand, and there will also be some storage space beneath the bench. The door and the sink will be along the wall separating the bathroom from the loft living area.

I put down chipboard flooring and there is space in the

bathroom for both of us to work. The bathroom is now separate; we refer to the rest of the loft as our building site. Dan had been busy with small nailing strips on the ceiling in the loft but now joins me in the bathroom.

We lower the ceiling and build the framework for the walls. The membrane on the floor is to run 8 inches up the walls, and will in turn be covered with moisture-resistant boards running right the way down to the cement floor. Now everything is ready for the membrane specialist, who is coming tomorrow.

This period of the project entails a lot of work on small surfaces. The bathroom, small nailing strips, and other things of a niggling nature take up most of the week, including all of Thursday. We continue at a slow pace; my patience is that of a saint now, Dan's no less so.

We work closely together and chat a lot between all the sundry tasks. This type of work is not particularly strenuous and makes for an enjoyable, relaxing week as long as we do not allow ourselves to be overcome by the feeling of getting little done.

Dan stays at home to do paperwork on Friday. The fumes from the membrane installation are not the best to breathe in and keeping away is no bad idea. I show up in the morning to show the specialist what needs to be done, after which the stairs carpenter comes by to take measurements. It takes the membrane man a while to get set up, so we make use of the time before the air becomes noxious.

Prior to leaving yesterday, Dan and I lifted away the chipboard covering the new stairwell. I remove the insulation before taking up the drywall sheets covering the small hole in the apartment ceiling downstairs, the one Dan and I used to get our dimensions. The stairs carpenter stands below and measures the height between the floor in the apartment and the floor in the loft, noting the distance to the millimeter. I replace the drywall sheets, fit the insulation back, and the stairs carpenter gives me a hand getting the chipboard back in place.

The fumes from the glue are becoming oppressive, so I head for home to catch up on some office work myself.

Later in the day I drop by to test the membrane by filling the bathroom floor with water. Before doing so I seal the drain with a balloon of sorts that is placed in the drain pipe and inflated. I take water from the apartment via a hose from the shower. The bathroom floor is turned into a mini swimming pool with four to six inches of water covering it, and will remain so overnight so we can be sure it is watertight.

Jon and Kari come up to take a look at the flooded bathroom floor, reassured no doubt that the waterproofing is being taken very seriously.

I pop in on Saturday afternoon. There is no hint that the water level has dropped or any other signs of leakage. I remove the balloon and drain the floor of water.

38

"IF YOU'RE NOT IN, YOU CAN'T WIN!" MY OLD BOSS GREW up with the sweepstakes and that was his usual greeting on a Monday morning. Now it is mine.

Bjørn Olav is putting in the underfloor heating on Tuesday and Johannes is pouring the bathroom floor on Wednesday. There will be no more carpentry done in the bathroom before the cement is set; we cannot run the risk of damaging either the membrane or the heating cables.

Dan twisted his knee skiing over the weekend, but he can still engage in light work. We put in the last of the nailing strips. I take care of the ones that are high up and awkward to get to, allowing Dan to keep to lower altitudes. His stiff knee and impaired mobility lead me to call him Long Dan Silver for the rest of the day. He is also told that there is little difference whether he has one good leg or two.

The skylights from Velux come with the option of a finished lining that can be fitted on-site. I do not like these and my clients in the city seldom opt for them. They have an institutional look about them, with a boring, white surface and soft curves instead of angled corners. What is more, they are surrounded with a trim where the lining meets the ceiling and I prefer the sharper lines you get with drywall. Visually, there is so much going on in an attic, with beams, a pitched roof, corners, and brickwork, so keeping it simple is the best option. We will in fact make the lining of the windows in drywall as I like, not that I am the one deciding. Kari and Jon want this solution.

There is a big difference in building culture between the city center and places just a twenty-minute drive away, which only increases the further you go. Velux lining kits are one example, being more popular the further you get from Oslo Central Station. The use of ceiling panels and MDF to imitate wood are two more examples of products more popular out of town. Painted drywall is viewed as a good thing in urban areas but seen as plain in the countryside.

There can be many reasons for these differences. Finances play a part. Housing is generally more reasonable, or less expensive, the farther you get from the city. Craftsmanship sometimes costs that much more than prefabricated solutions, so the city dweller is more likely to spend a little extra money on a costly apartment than the person living where the price per square foot is lower.

The construction business also plays a part. There are not only more customers in cities, as well as a greater variation of them, there are also more tradesmen. The breadth of expertise is then increased, leading to a greater range of things they can do than would be found in a small place with few tradesmen.

It also has to do with taste. There are more people in urban areas with higher education and so-called cultural capital. They do not want plain domiciles, and MDF is regarded as plain in those circles. Paradoxically, bare, white plastered walls are considered plain by many of those living a short train ride away from the new, white opera house in the center of Oslo.

Personally I prefer plaster but I can sympathize with those in the MDF camp. I live in Tøyen, in the east of the city, but am originally from the provinces, so you could say I am torn between two cultures. Still, as a tradesman I have an overriding affinity for craftsmanship and the person paying me to carry it out. The most important thing about a home is that the people living in it have somewhere to hang their hat, as they say, and that they are happy there.

The nailing strips for the window lining are not that easy to get into place. The ceiling, now insulated, is of considerable thickness, and the window lining is deep. We splay the sides, increasing the width of the opening in the interior to allow in more light. The top is horizontal and the bottom is perpendicular. The end result could remind you of an embrasure on a castle battlement.

We cut drywall to the angles the lining will have and place these templates in the grooves for the lining, placing our nail strips according to these templates. In doing one we will have angles of the linings for all the windows.

The lining should look good, but insulation is also needed around the windows, and our splayed sides mean less room for that. We compensate for this by using the flexible steel band for the nail strips. The steel takes no space from the insulation, is quick to work with, and is precise.

Details like the nailing strips for the windows take a lot of time and it can appear to clients as though our work is at a standstill. I like to do these smaller jobs as they arise, while Dan is often more impatient and eager to press ahead. For him it is more appealing to wait with the bits and bobs, working instead on what yields greater visual results. As long as we are productive it is much of a muchness what we do, but I think getting the detailed work done as it crops up and getting it out of the way gives a better overview. It is boring to busy yourself with it for too long at a time, so spreading it out is preferable.

The clients are not present while we work and do not see what we are doing. The work that takes longest is also often work the clients do not understand needs doing. They might then think we are letting them down, that we are not in place and on the job. So I will always make sure to keep them informed about what we are actually up to, maybe even exaggerate how tired and frustrated we are at how long things are taking.

If it is work that is billed by the hour, then it is even more important to make the client understand that we are actually hard at it. I have, on occasion, wound up in conflict with customers on account of them not seeing or understanding the work I have carried out. Any kind of invoice can then seem unreasonably large. Is it my fault for not managing to make it clear to them? Maybe, but it is not that easy explaining things to people when they do not really understand them.

The Petersens have been good at asking questions along the way and considering carefully the problems they have faced. They have taken the bull by the horns and made decisions when it has been necessary. Whenever I have wanted to show them what we are busy with they have come to take a look, so we are on the same page.

Kari and Jon are coming, together with Herlovsen, the architect. They wanted him to cast an eye over the work thus far, as an extra assurance that things are being done properly. His visit will give the Petersens an independent, professional view of the most important work. I have made it clear I would appreciate a visit. We have spoken a few times on the telephone and I have explained how things are going and described some of the solutions we have chosen as we have progressed. After having talked to the Petersens and me he does not think it necessary to come, and views everything as under control. It costs money after all; he charges site visits at an hourly rate, and as such it is an unnecessary expense if everything is OK. But Kari and Jon still wanted him to come and take a look, saying it would serve to put their minds at ease.

Herlovsen and I discuss what we see around us in the loft and on the photographs I have taken, while Kari and Jon listen and ask questions now and again. We pay particular attention to the support structure, bathroom, and the knee wall since this is work hidden to the eye that will have the greatest consequences if it is not done properly. The photographs are handy to have now.

Portions of the work were agreed after the architect had done his drawings, so Herlovsen is given a run-through of the solutions chosen, the interior decoration of the bathroom, the aspen paneling to go on the ceiling, the customized Ikea furnishings on the mezzanine, and so on. He says it is going to turn out nicely and the tradesman is given the blessing of the architect for work done so far. There remains a lot to do but we are progressing nicely and according to plan. We are heading in the right direction. The client can relax.

For me, this can be viewed as marketing. The fact that Herlovsen has seen firsthand the work we have carried out could lead him to recommend us to his clients. Assuming he likes it.

39

WHILE DAN AND I ARE BUSY WITH THE NAILING strips, Bjørn Olav arrives to lay the cables for the underfloor heating in the bathroom. Once finished, he goes on to install tubing for the electrics in the ceiling. This tubing already has wiring inside, so he will avoid feeding that through later on. He easily positions these over the 2×4s in the dropped ceiling, clamping them into place so they do not dangle or droop.

If electrical conduits are installed too near the perimeter of a structure, close to the cold in a wall or roof, the air within them may become too cool and moisture will condense. This is tantamount to water leakage, which may find its way into a junction box. In this case, the insulating layer around the conduits that might otherwise be exposed to cold is so thick that there is no danger of that.

Wherever outlets, for power points, sockets, or lights, are to be placed, Bjørn has fitted boxes that the tubes are led toward. There is an entire network to keep track of, in addition to controlling the circuits they are connected to. The regulations for electrical installation are no breeze either.

I always tell electricians they have an easy job; it is only plus and minus, after all. It is, of course, not easy, but they do deserve a bit of stick, as punishment for all the bits of wiring they leave strewn about. My theory is that they are actively taught not to tidy up from the very first day on their training course.

The Petersens have heeded the advice about having enough outlets to avoid extension leads and they also want all the old wiring in the apartment redone. They will have an upgraded electrical system when Bjørn Olav is finished.

Johannes and Gustav, his apprentice, arrive on Wednesday with their forced-action mixer. It is a heavy piece of equipment but there are two of them, so they manage it OK. Johannes is happy that the materials they are going to use have already been lifted up by crane, but Gustav is probably happier still, since he is the one who would no doubt have done most of the carrying.

I am not sure whether the bricklayer or carpenter has the more strenuous occupation within the construction trades, but the lot of the bricklayer is not an easy one, and involves a lot of lifting and carrying. I view our two trades as brothers, along with the metalworkers. Or perhaps we are sisters? Our fields have long traditions and much in common, both physically and technically.

A forced-action mixer is relatively wieldy on smaller jobs like this. The machine mixes the cement well and that is important. A lot of bathrooms have been built where the bricklayer poured water into the sack and thought the mixture good enough as long as the contents were sufficiently moist. That does not turn out well.

A mistake in the amount of water in relation to cement can have serious consequences, and it is also important to take temperature into consideration. The cement can harden too quickly, leading to the edges raising, lifting where the cement meets walls. The contents of the sacks can also vary, so even using a measuring bucket is no guarantee of getting it right. You need to be able to see that the cement is mixed correctly.

These are all important concerns, and if more mistakes are made it only compounds the problem. This is an example of the knowledge that comes gradually and in some cases at a high price, both for the individual tradesman and for the trade itself.

Mistakes are about more than building lopsided or out of plumb. The bricklayer works with chemistry, not wholly dissimilar to the chef and his sauces.

They lay the cement with a slope toward the drains and make a depression in the shower approximately a tile's thickness deep. Johannes is in control of everything, while the apprentice is there to learn. Johannes lifts the wire mesh up in the cement layer so that it lies in the middle. This is important in terms of reinforcement and for the heating cables to have good effect when warming up the cement layer. The poured bed needs to be packed properly. Any air pockets can lead to the cables within overheating and being damaged.

Johannes lays a sheet of plastic over the floor to allow the mix to harden correctly and not dry out too fast. Tomorrow we will water the floor, moisten the cement, and put the plastic sheeting back over it.

40

ON THURSDAY I RENT A CHERRY PICKER TO ALLOW US to install the three vent covers on the roof and the grilles on the air holes in the knee wall. This needs to be carried out now before we insulate and seal the roof internally.

While I collect the cherry picker, Dan makes holes in the roof where the covers are to be located. He can do this from inside. He cuts and removes the roof boards but leaves the rest until I return. The roof slates rest upon battens, running horizontally, and counter battens, going vertically, and when the roof board underneath is taken away, he is able to jiggle the slates aside from within the attic and remove what is needed of both types of battens. I will be down on the street making sure nobody walks by below while he does this. A roof slate falling on the head of a passerby is a bad advertisement for us. We have learned that without attending a course.

Because of my fear of heights it is up to Dan to man the cherry picker. He is fearless, at least in my eyes. I am glad he can do those jobs that are high up, because I could never go up in the basket of the boom, no matter what you paid me.

While he is up there I stay inside supplying him with the materials and tools he needs through the holes in the roof.

The covers, boxes in plywood, are finished and ready to go on. We mount them securely and at the correct angle.

Petter, the metalworker, comes to take measurements from the roof covers for the additional sheathing. He will make these at the workshop, returning tomorrow to adjust them to the roof slates and mount them. In the meantime we cover the boxes with roofing felt, another measure to make sure the roof is safely sealed. Dan also puts the grilles in place for the ventilation holes in the knee wall.

Petter returns on Friday morning and finishes off the work on the roof. He takes the cherry picker with him when he leaves and will deliver it back to the hire company on his way home. It was good to get all that out of the way.

The cement has hardened sufficiently for us to start work in the bathroom again.

The knee wall in the bathroom will be a double wall and is important to build right. The furthest wall is insulated and covered with polyethylene like the rest of the attic, and on the inside of this we will build the bathroom wall. So we have a bathroom wall and a wall against the elements. No insulation will be placed between these walls, and the cavity between the two layers must be well ventilated or damp will accumulate. Before we close off the walls and ceiling, the plumber and electrician carry out their work.

The water pipes will be placed between these two walls. These will be led into a junction box for water. From this cabinet, which functions as a sort of fuse box for water, the pipes will run to the different installations in the bathroom.

The water travels through a pipe-in-pipe system. This consists of two separate pipes where the actual carrier pipe is enclosed within a second pipe, and should a leak occur in the inner pipe, the outer jacket pipe will catch it. All the pipes are connected in the cabinet and any potential leak will appear here and be led out over the bathroom floor to the drain. Provided Thomas does not mess it up and no one damages both pipes with a screw or something similar, there ought not to be any leaks with a system like this. It is also possible to reinsert or change out the inner pipe, should it be necessary. Avoiding having to tear out walls or rip up flooring to repair a water pipe is a good thing.

Every now and then one of us will head down to Strøm Larsen and buy a hot lunch or some other kind of treat. Today it is Dan's turn to bicycle down to one of the best delicatessens in town, so he gets to choose what is on the menu, which turns out to be tasty sausages and potato salad. Norwegians do not eat a hot meal for lunch very often, so we feel like Swedes for a while, and not a little envious too. Every time, we agree to do this much more often but seldom do. Hot food on proper plates, with real cutlery from the Petersens' kitchen, it turns into a long lunch.

41

I HAD PLANNED TO PUT UP MOISTURE-RESISTANT BOARDS on the brick walls at each end of the bathroom. The walls are not level and require straightening. These boards would have solved that problem but we would have had to use a thicker variant, which would have taken up space and are not inexpensive. Instead Johannes suggested that his apprentice, Gustav, be given the opportunity to render the walls and straighten them out that way. He needs to learn how to plaster, so we cannot let the opportunity pass by. It is important that apprentices get the chance to carry out a variety of work, particularly in smaller firms. Time and a lot of different work tasks are needed to learn the trade. Small firms have few projects at a time and have to organize them in a smart way if apprentices are to gain a broad breadth of experience. This plastering job is good training, as the walls are to be tiled afterward, meaning there is no need for a finer, finishing coat.

The first layer of mortar, the so-called rough coat, is applied by throwing mortar on the wall, and the job is completed with a finishing coat. If the first coat is not done properly the whole job will be poor; there can be bubbling above, cavities beneath, or it can crack. The quality of the finishing coat is visible to everyone. Gustav can learn about fine plastering later; in the meantime he can practice on the first coat.

Johannes tells us about sundried bricks from Mesopotamia made to a standardized measurement. Brick manufacture must be one of the first examples of modern industrial production.

Bricks vary in size but are relatively similar and there are two main reasons for that. The bricklayer needs to be able to hold the brick in one hand to leave his other free to wield the trowel. The mason must be able to lift thousands of them without suffering an injury. The human physique has dictated their size and weight, so both aesthetics and health and safety have a part to play in this instance.

In addition, the ratio between the length and width of the bricks or blocks is such that it works out mathematically when they are being laid, so the brain was also involved in determining their size.

The architect who designed Oslo City Hall wanted larger bricks than the standard. At the beginning, the bricklayers laid the bricks as normal, but upon suffering from tendinitis and similar complaints they had to stop working as usual and use two hands for each block. The City Hall is a wonderful building and part of this is no doubt down to the size of the bricks, but it must have taken a lot of time to cover the facade with all that brickwork.

Johannes works with the same tools they used to build the Tower of Babel, a stonemason's hammer and plumb bob. We have some equipment in common, like the chalk line and the carpenter's variant on the hammer. The ax is my "ur-tool." It is the same in principle whether made from flint, bronze, or steel. Our most basic tools are the same: our bodies.

If Johannes had traveled a few thousand years back in time

he could have fitted straight into a work crew helping build the original Tower of Babel.

Speaking the language might have made things easier for him, or on second thought perhaps not, if you are to believe the story. Still, he would not need to understand the language, or in this case languages. The expertise he has in his field would have cut right through the chaos. And knowing Johannes, within a month he would be regarded as a well-respected colleague.

Gustav plasters the walls. It will take a few days, seeing as several layers need to be applied. We will then spread a breathable membrane over it, and tiles can be placed right onto that. Johannes can begin tiling on Monday next week.

Since the plastering is being done in stages, Dan and I can work on the bathroom in between. First we put up boarding on the other walls. We cut wet-room boards to size and mount them on top of the paneling, fit adhesive patches with sleeves on all the pipes and electrical outlets, and apply sealant tape in the corners. Dan spreads the membrane coating on the walls in the places where it is needed.

Thomas arrives to install the toilet casing and set up the bathtub. I build a recessed casing around the wall-hung toilet, covering it with moisture-resistant boards. It is important to have a floor-level opening in the casing so that the water can run out should the toilet leak. The casing, like the knee wall, needs to be free of moisture and damp, so a vent valve is placed on top. We use valves actually designed for boats, small, elegant ones in stainless steel.

While we are working in the bathroom, Dan goes out to collect some materials and calls out to me, saying the place is haunted. The handle on the stairwell door is jiggling slightly but no one is coming in. Then it stops, before once again moving up and down. Dan summons the courage to walk over and open the door. He is met by the sight of Fredrik, looking slightly scared and teary-eyed.

"Goodness, if it isn't the building inspector back again."

Fredrik begins to bawl and Dan picks him up.

"Have you come up to visit us all on your own?"

"Yes," he replies, having difficulty speaking through the sobs.

"What about Mamma and Pappa and Jens, are they downstairs maybe? Mamma and Pappa are probably wondering where you are, don't you think?"

"Yes, but I just wanted to look. At the loft, and our room."

"I think we should go down and tell them you've been up here all on your own. Maybe they'd like to come up too; let's you and me ask them. Come on."

Kari and Jon get a surprise when Dan and Fredrik appear. They had forgotten to lock the door. Fredrik begins to cry again; it is no doubt a little frightening being off on an expedition alone, especially without permission.

"We thought maybe everyone would like to come up and take a look?" Dan says.

They would indeed, so Dan asks their patience for about an hour so that we can finish up for the day—for the week—in fact, seeing as it is Friday afternoon. They go along with that.

One hour later, Fredrik enters with Jens close on his heels. They bring us a plate of buns that Fredrik carries with arms outstretched. Freshly baked currant buns. We have a building meeting with buns and then we are off for the weekend.

42

WE SAY HELLO ON MONDAY MORNING AND GET THE NEW week under way. Kari and Jon have decided they want us to carry out the work that was earmarked as optional for them to do themselves when we signed the contract. They think the building has been enough hassle as it is. The thought of having to embark on a fresh round of renovation themselves after we have finished is probably not that tempting.

We are ready to insulate the roof. Above our dropped ceiling we will put in an 8-inch layer across the nailing strips and then a second layer of 4 inches between the nailing strips in the dropped ceiling, so 12 in total. The ceiling between the apartment and loft was poorly insulated, so even though the apartment floorage will soon double, the heating bills will not increase.

It is the middle of April but it is still chilly in the attic; spring comes late to buildings under construction. The sun is not strong enough to heat up inside but at night the cold seeps in, making the attic like a Thermos that retains the cold. Once we get the first layer of insulation in place the heating can be switched on. It will not take much more than that to make this loft a far more pleasant place to work.

Insulation needs to be put in properly. Attractive insulation is effective insulation, as my old boss used to say. Cutting corners and shoddy installation is not good and can result in thermal bridges and even problems with condensation in the ceiling. It is yet another example of important work that can be underestimated. There is a big difference between someone who knows what they are doing and someone who does not. Those who can do the job end up with attractive and even insulation, without holes or wastage, and are able to carry out the work a lot quicker.

Wearing a mask will exclude most of the dust from insulation that can get to the lungs, but fibers can also cause the skin to react. We have outfits we can wear but I only use them when it is really bad. I think they are too clammy and uncomfortable.

Insulation has improved greatly. The old fiberglass matting from the 1950s is a nightmare to work with on renovation jobs, especially in the heat of the summer. Some people have almost an allergic reaction to modern insulation, but fortunately I have no problem with it. There is also a certain degree of psychology at play. If you think about it itching then the itch becomes unbearable. If you manage to put it out of your mind then working with insulation can be quite pleasant, with the radio on and the sound becoming warmer as the insulation progresses in the room. Music sounds better in those soft surroundings, violins and electric guitars in particular.

A shower after a day spent putting in insulation is high on the list of the best showers you can ever experience. First cold water to close the pores and rinse away the fibers, followed by a good scrub with hot water.

A new day of heavy lifting with the crane, the last one on this job, and there is so little to come up that Dan and I can handle it on our own. I have been following the weather forecast lately and if they had predicted rain I would have postponed the lift. We are bringing in flooring, planks, trim, and casing, none of which can get damp.

The wooden materials will now be left for a week or two, allowing them time to acclimatize to the interior of the loft. Wood needs to adjust to the natural relative humidity inside, so it is important we have the heating on and achieve a balanced temperature similar to how it will be when the attic is used. If the materials do not adapt to the loft, cracks may appear in the joints, between the floorboards, and in the seams between skirting board and the like.

It is said that wood is a living material, and the moisture content is of particular importance. There is a world of difference between damp and dry wood. A floor plank can be 4 inches in width when dry and 4.25 when moist.

We are also lifting up the materials we will use to make the bathroom fixtures. Waste and rubble is lowered down, along with tools and items no longer needed. From now on anything going up or down will have to go via the stairs. When the last of the materials has been taken in through the hole in the roof we close it up and put in the final window. Once we are finished with the flashings around the window all the exterior work is done.

While Dan and I are busy loading and unloading, Johannes and the apprentice are tiling the bathroom. They start with the floor.

The layout, how the tiles are distributed, is important. There should be, in as far as it is possible, equally sized tiles at each endpoint on the floor, not one whole tile on one side and a narrow piece on the other. The distribution of tiles on the floor should suit the distribution of the tiles on the walls, and this is easier to accomplish when you start with the floor.

To achieve an overall result that looks good, Johannes has to take the floor, walls, toilet, bathtub, and shower area into consideration. There are a lot of variables.

We are ready to cover the dropped ceiling in polyethylene sheeting. It is to be put in place such that all the joints are hugged tightly and all seams are sealed. However, the surface of the gable wall is so uneven it is not possible to manage this.

We staple the sheeting securely to the nailing strips with a staple gun, being careful to hold the plastic taut so it sits evenly. We apply an appropriate amount of construction adhesive to the brick wall between the plastic and the wall. We can now press the plastic hard against the adhesive to seal it completely. If we fail to do this, air leaks will occur along the entire wall, increasing the risk of condensation, in turn leading to mold and rot and all the misery that entails.

We place adhesive patches on all the openings in the plastic, augmenting with tape where necessary. Around the window linings we use the vapor barriers provided by Velux. We had covered the area above the beam in polyethylene before lifting it into place beneath the roof rafters, having already taken care of the area from the mezzanine floor and up, and now have a roof that is well sealed against moisture from the inside climate.

We are going to drywall the ceiling on Monday, so we spend the rest of the day preparing for that. We tidy the floor to give the traveling scaffolding space to move, stack the drywall on the saw horses, fetch a plaster square and an extra-long spirit level, and change the blades on the Stanley knives. Dan has a drywall lift that will help us somewhat, although we can only use it on parts of the ceiling. The height of the roof ridge rules out using it there, so that will require us lifting by hand, and down at the knee wall it is too low to get the plasterboard lift underneath.

Fifty-seven pounds is not too heavy a weight for two people to lift, but the boards are rather fragile, and holding them up over our heads until we have screwed them tightly is awkward and laborious. A static load, like holding a board above your head, can be strenuous. We will need to work quickly and efficiently to avoid holding the boards any longer than necessary.

It is all in the technique, which if you have not mastered, is like trying to lift the whole roof. You will press the board unnecessarily hard against the nailing strips, at the same time as you are trying to use your other hand to operate the drill. The house is heavy, so you are not going to lift it no matter how hard you try. Practice is what is required, and technique.

My old boss was not too impressed the first time we lifted drywall up to a ceiling and he saw how panicky and tired I was while he remained calm and relaxed. You're younger than me, he said, but I'm older than you, and he was absolutely right. I am older now.

The weekend has come at the right time; it means I can have a rest before we lift the drywall up to the ceiling. Dan and I are both older and wiser in the job, but it is still hard work.

43

MONDAY MORNING.

We are now at the phase of the project where it is imperative that we keep up the pace, get things done. Insulating, plastering, floor laying, this type of work is about volume, square feet. The work will be carried out properly, but the difference between passing off something as progress and making real headway is big. These weeks are physically tiring. A lot of lifting, constantly in motion, up and down.

So the volume on the radio must be cranked up; music is needed and lots of it. Music can be like fuel for the machinery, although when they play something awful we turn it down. We do not want sand in the works.

There is a lot left to do but the hours required to complete it all are less than one might imagine. I explain this to Kari and Jon. It is now just past the middle of April and we are well on schedule.

Before covering the roof in plastic sheeting, we transferred a chalk line onto a nailing strip, and the first row of drywall will be laid along this straight line.

The gable wall is coarsely plastered and has large and small bulges and hollows. The first board is screwed up provisionally and can now be adjusted to fit the uneven surface.

Using a pencil, I draw on the board, following the wall and its bumps, depressions, and inconsistencies. This method of drawing on a material is called scribing. The word alone makes working with gypsum easier and less tiresome. It is a beautiful word, closely linked to art and craft.

I have now drawn the shape of the wall on the board. Using a Stanley knife I cut the gypsum. Usually you would make an incision through the paper on one side of the board, allowing you to snap it along the incision and cut through the paper layer on the other side. That is possible along a straight line but not when I am adjusting the board to the brick wall. I could have sawed along the line with a rat-tail file but a knife is just as quick and gives a better result. The side of the board is sharper than the slightly fuzzy edge the saw would give. The knife involves a little more effort but is manageable.

Many carpenters use a snap-off knife when working on gypsum, but they are not as good to work with. The difference is particularly apparent now when cutting freehand along the uneven line I have inscribed.

The classic Stanley knife is an example of a manufacturer becoming so dominant that the brand name is now synonymous with the tool. When used properly their knife demonstrates a number of advantages compared with poorer-quality alternatives. Arguments about snap knives versus Stanley knives can become quite heated when I discuss them with those who favor the former. In my opinion, they have either not learned what is best or do not care enough if they use a painting and decorating tool for carpentry.

Once I have finished cutting the drywall, we mount it along the chalk line and screw it tightly. It sits nicely, with a distance of between 5 mm and 10 mm to the wall to leave room for the filler. This material between joints must be even to look good, and the sharply cut edge from the Stanley knife will now be part of the finish. A narrow joint is more liable to crack than a wider one. There must be enough width for the filler to stretch and expand a little with the movements in the construction, in the same way as a longer elastic band tolerates more motion than a shorter one.

After the ceiling surfaces are plastered, the windows remain like unfinished parts of a drawing. It took a long time to make the nailing strips for the linings but making the drywall is faster. We make a template and copy the linings window by window; it looks as if the ceiling falls into place.

The drywall work is one of the parts of the job that most change the appearance of the attic. It is starting to look like it could be a nice place to live in. The acoustics again become harder but the even surfaces and more pronounced lines make the space calmer. The films in my head roll; they become ceilings, walls, floors, and windows. The clips become a whole, an experience physically measurable, where imagination and reality have now almost melded, theory into practice.

The family pay us a Friday visit. The boys are familiar with the loft now, view it as their own as they run around. Their mother and father calm them down a little and I tell them they can draw on the drywall if they like. It is the largest canvas they have ever seen. Dan sharpens carpenter pencils for them and they get started. It takes a little time before they understand how much space is at their disposal. Drawing high up on the ceiling, while Dan watches them on the ladder, is the high point. Fredrik is good at making plans for what they will draw, and Jens, who has some ideas of his own, is coopted. They draw houses, with rooms and household objects, suns, stars, and trees. Their father impresses everyone by drawing a huge bird flying among the stars. They ask if they can fetch their color markers from downstairs but are not allowed; they might show through the paint if they are the wrong type. But making do with pencils seems fun enough all the same.

With the children busy we adults have a chance to talk. There is nothing problematic we need to discuss; the work is coming along. We chat about how it will be; if it is turning out the way they had hoped. They probably think it seems smaller than they had envisaged, but we explain that it will open up again once finished. A tidy room without a load of materials and tools, with painted ceiling and walls, will appear larger than this building site.

We explain a little about the order of work yet to be done and how long the different tasks will take. The boys want to carry on drawing but relent when they hear that they can continue tomorrow.

"Have a nice weekend, everyone."

44

"'MORNING, ALL."

Monday, the start of a new week, and I greet everyone downstairs.

Jens and Fredrik have been busy over the weekend. Their parents have swept the floor and made a bit of room to make it easier for them to pursue their artistic endeavors, and they have drawn high and low, on a large and small scale. There are a number of animals, some of the species slightly hard to determine, but there is a horse Pippi would have envied them. They have drawn a block of flats that starts down at the floor and continues over the knee wall up onto the ceiling, with curtains and flowerpots in the windows. Fredrik has drawn my van down on the knee wall, at the side of the building. They know my van by sight now since their mom and dad have pointed out the carpenter's car on the way to and from school.

Bjørn Olav comes and connects the wires and inner components in his boxes. He will wait to install the actual sockets, switches, and the like until after the painter is finished. We want easier access to electricity, though, so he finishes off two of the sockets all the same and connects up one of the circuits to the loft in the fuse box. It is nice to get rid of the leads that have been strewn around and stick a plug straight into a socket in the wall.

It is a bit messy after the plastering, so Dan and I give the place a thorough tidy and set up the carpentry equipment. We put the table saw and miter saw, or drop saw, in place but out of the way of our work. We set up the plunge saw we use to cut boards and fix a newly sharpened blade on it. We are going to do finer work now and the blade has to be honed.

The painters come after lunch to prep the walls. I rang them last week when we were well under way putting up drywall so they would have time to put the job into their schedule.

The painters are considerate, working around us and our materials with hardly any mess. They cover up where it is necessary. Ideally we would not be here while they are but we are eager to press on and do not have any other jobs to go to, so we just have to put up with each other. It is often that way at the end of projects like this one, lots happening at the same time, some of us on ladders, others on their knees. When everyone is thoughtful and makes allowances a lot of people doing their thing at the same time like this can be a pleasant experience.

Johannes and Gustav are finished tiling the bathroom and it is now ready for us. The aspen ceiling on the bathroom is a nice little number that Dan gets. We split the enjoyable tasks too, just as much as we split the tiring or boring ones. There is quite a difference between working with boarding in the bathroom and tidying away heavy materials.

Untreated boards of aspen are one of my favorites, especially in a bathroom. The wood is light with a velvety feel. When I see an aspen board like this I want to touch it, caress it. It also soaks up moisture well, making it ideal for a bathroom. Good ventilation and underfloor heating will make this the driest room in the apartment, but it will undergo large fluctuations in humidity. Part of the damp from a hot shower will be absorbed by the aspen and released over time as ventilation dries the room. The tiles, like the mirror, are covered with a film of condensation, and it makes for a damp feeling in the room after a shower. Aspen boards balance this. It is not a very expensive solution compared to the cost of spackled and painted drywall and molding around the ceiling.

Wood is beautiful when used right, and the memories people may have of "the hell" of pine interiors in the 1970s should not blind them to all the other ways it can be used. Hardwood does not often feature in construction. We have pine and spruce in our DNA, so hardwood is usually relegated to firewood. Producers are trying to develop hardwood products on a national scale and convince customers that the wood is excellent for all kinds of applications, both indoors and outdoors.

We have a lot of wood in this country and its production is environmentally friendly. One advantage of this raw material is it gives such scope on a domestic level for further processing, we do not have to be just producers of a commodity. This is of course dependent upon our expertise, that we have tradesmen who can deliver good work to the customers. The forester, sawmill worker, timber trader, and tradesman. Dan and I are the final link in a chain that begins with forestry. If the chain is broken it is to the detriment of all.

The bathroom ceiling is quite small, so it does not take long to get the tongue-and-groove boards in place. Dan makes a nice plain molding in aspen where the wood meets the walls. It looks just as we hoped it would: tasteful, bright, and airy.

While Dan has been busy with the ceiling, I have been making the bathroom furniture, almost as though it were a model kit. I am constructing it in 1.5-inch thick, oiled counter-top oak. It will be simple and beautiful, and although it is furniture making, the work is not complicated.

BATHROOM FURNITURE

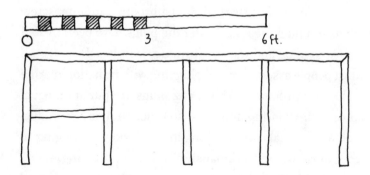

There will be two pieces, one on either side of the bathroom, neither of them with doors. The idea is for the two of them to be jointed to supports, standing on the floor like legs. These supports, or sides, are in the same worktop material.

I make a miter joint, cutting the ends of the supports and surface to fit at a 45-degree angle, making sure the corners look nice and tight. I will put in wooden biscuits, and glue and screw the parts together into a strong, stable construction. Everything is screwed tight and the final adhesive applied when it is in place in the bathroom.

The screws I use for fastening tight the pieces are hidden by wooden plugs. I bore 10 mm holes in the wood, then I make plugs the same size to put in the holes to hide the screws. This will be an important part of the finish of both pieces of furniture.

Beneath one will be a washing machine and a tumble dryer separated by an upright, and also space for a linen basket and one final area divided by a shelf. The oak I use for the supports also doubles as the walls between these areas.

The washstand will go on the wall opposite, and will also be made from worktop material, but on a smaller scale with only one shelf.

I assemble the furniture in the bathroom and glue, screw together, and plug the holes. After the plugs have been treated with a blend of oil and wax the furniture is finished.

Most people associate wood plugging with imitation marine deck flooring in houses. The ersatz plugs are put at an equal distance in the flooring, but serve no function. It is a reproduction of what I make with my hands and tools, belonging to another world where workmanship is window dressing.

On actual boat decks, wooden plugs, or bungs, are a good

solution: screws fasten planks to the structure beneath and the bungs prevent moisture from penetrating the decking through the screw holes. Whenever I see replica decking I always think of Aker Brygge and the expensive apartments on the waterfront in Oslo. There is supposed to be something maritime about these apartment blocks built on an old ship-yard, with a view over the marina. Whether it is an attempt to mimic the deck of a luxury yacht or of a barge is hard to say. For me bungs are a simple and fast way of jointing that looks good and customers like.

45

THOMAS COMES TO INSTALL THE MIXER TAP AND connect everything up in the bathroom. Now everything in there is ready for use but we will refrain from smirching it and rather let the Petersens enjoy the pleasure of their brand-new bathroom. In any case we are accustomed to using the one downstairs, and the Petersens are used to us going up and down, so it will be fine for another couple of weeks.

Dan puts in the bathroom door and doorframe. He also makes a frame around the door to the stairwell. He puts the casing in place using a minimum of nails, without hammering them all the way in, so we can disassemble it before finally fixing it after the floor is laid.

We invite Thomas and the painters down to the kitchen for lunch. With so many people in their working clothes in the Petersens' cozy kitchen, it is a little like being in a luxurious workmen's shed-cum-eatery. The painters prepare their food upstairs and take it down with them. Thomas is a plumber, but he eats an electrician's lunch: buns and a soft drink. Dan and I help ourselves to our provisions in the refrigerator. Thomas does not want real food and keeps to what he is used to. It is a culinary clash of cultures between the Vietnamese painters, the carpenters on long-term contract, and plumbers who work to order.

The Petersens want some Ikea furnishings in the loft and would like us to assemble them. They are planning to use the mezzanine floor as an office space. They want low cabinets running in the direction of the roof on one side, which will also be like a little knee wall, making the area feel more like a room of its own. A roof coming right to the floor can make a place feel cramped, as well as being problematic when cleaning. The other side of the mezzanine, facing the boys' bedroom, needs to be closed off. On that side we will build the mezzanine floor further out to the sloped roof, and that will also serve as the ceiling in the bedroom. We will erect a small knee wall, 8 inches high, on that side of the "office."

At the far end, against the firewall, they want floor-to-ceiling shelving, and that will have to be adjusted to fit the decrease in width the higher it goes.

Dan makes nailing strips for the extension of the mezzanine floor. He drywalls underneath, insulates and places chipboard on top. I customize the Ikea cabinets that will follow the slope of the roof. There is less space when they are sawed to fit but that is still better than nothing. I adjust the shelving to fit the firewall, then we clear everything from the mezzanine and lay the floor. We assemble the cabinets and fix them and the shelving into place, put up the skirting board, and the mezzanine is finished. We get the feeling that we are quite literally working our way out of the loft, even though there remains much left to do.

Kari and Jon had a pretty clear idea of how they wanted their new conversion furnished. What we are making is a variation on what they had in mind. At first they were surprised by my suggestions. They thought, for example, that the custom-made bathroom furniture would be much more expensive than the

Ikea items they had planned on. I am often asked what I think of Ikea. Kari and Jon wondered the same thing. As though Ikea is something specific, something measurable, like a ceiling height, the dimensions of a window, or the size of a living space.

Ikea is everywhere. The quality is consistent with most of the stuff that people buy for their homes, regardless of name or brand. It is simple and relatively inexpensive, and you get what you pay for.

For the Petersens and other consumers, the interiors they find in catalogs are part of a predictable universe, a bit like the gravity that keeps all of us on the ground. I understand this side of the experience and have Ikea articles at home myself but view them with indifference. They are mostly hidden behind or beneath nicer items I own. I make maximum use of their functionality but prefer not having them in plain sight.

The furniture Ikea makes is intended to last for a short time compared with, for instance, something sturdy made in oak or a solid wood floor. Ikea is so prevalent and occupies such a strong place that I sometimes wonder if it has affected our idea of time, or if it is merely a result of the times we live in. The need to replace an object is a result of the quality of that object, but can also be a reason for the quality. Why build something that lasts when people will grow tired of it and change it after a short time anyway? The short-term, inter-changeable nature of these objects makes it difficult to relate to them in a satisfactory way. I am, however, glad that a distinc-tion in quality exists, where I represent the other side, an alternative with an understandable, intrinsic value. The danger is that whereas Ikea previously used to imitate craft and workmanship, we now find ourselves starting to mimic Ikea.

It is a situation that will not be favorable for the likes of me in the long run.

Funnily enough I am off to Ikea tonight, so I cannot avoid the place this week, not even in my spare time. If you own a van people often ask for your help in moving things. For me, the weekend means a rest from physical work, but for other people it means time to transport things; I risk becoming a moving service in my leisure time. I could easily spend ten to fifteen Saturdays a year on this, but I consistently say no, so not too many people ask anymore. Ole is always there for me, so I have agreed to help him, but I have said that making me go to Ikea is a sure way of putting our friendship to the test. There will, however, be Swedish meatballs for dinner tonight. Ole's treat.

46

I NEED TO DROP BY MY ACCOUNTANT IN CONNECTION with my tax returns. Being self-employed means I submit them in May. Dan is at the Petersens' and will start the new working week without me. Once finished with the accountant, I am happy and relieved. Let the week begin.

We have three big jobs left to do. First we will lay the floor, after that we will build the bedroom wall, and then we will make the new opening for the stairs.

We usually wear sturdy, steel-toe boots but change to lighter shoes now, without a pattern on the soles, for indoor wear. We need to avoid small stones getting stuck underneath, and the soles of the lighter ones do not streak the floor or leave scuff marks.

We begin laying the floor at the knee wall. The distribution has to be right, ending nicely at all the walls, with floorboards of good width. There also needs to be a gap between the boards and the walls so the wood can shrink and expand along with the temperature and humidity in the room. If the flooring is placed too tightly against the walls it can end up expanding so much it pushes the walls outward. Although it is more likely the walls stand firm, making the floor buckle somewhere in the middle.

The joints need to be distributed so that they do not line up, or come too close, and thus make a visible pattern. Some of the boards are damaged or have unsightly knots. To lay the floor more quickly we sort the boards into different lengths and make four stacks, from short to long. We can then choose which one we want according to how our joints are looking; at the same time we put the damaged boards aside as we progress.

We adjust and fit three rows of boards lengthwise in the room at a time before putting them down and screwing them tight. It gives us a kind of mass production effect and saves time, as well as making it easier to get a nice pattern with the joints, knots, and appearance of the boards. A well-laid floor is much more attractive than a floor with no thought put into it.

We knock the boards into place with a hammer and a tapping block before screwing them down. Many times we need to use a wood chisel to fit them together. We knock the chisel hard against the underlying chipboard floor and pry the tapping block to push the board into place. Putting down a floor is a time-consuming task but fine as long as you work steadily. However, your back, shoulders, and knees do not thank you.

The radio is on and what Dan and I are engaged in can seem like a dance of sorts. We hardly ever stand on each other's toes. I take a look at what he is doing and use the saw while he puts a floorboard down. He comes over to help if I am having trouble with a longer, stubborn board without my needing to ask, before getting back to his own thing. We talk while working, about the music we are listening to, about the news, all sorts of things but very little about work. That is limited to brief comments and quick questions, and that is all that is needed. It is a pleasant way of working.

We lay the floor over the edges of the hole for the stairs and mark the floor half an inch farther out than where the chipboard is etched for cutting. When the floor is laid past the mark and over the hole, we cut it with a plunge saw according to our markings. With a good blade on the saw we get a perfect edge.

Later, the drywall we will put up on the sides of the stairwell will fit neatly beneath our little ledge. All that is needed is a very simple skirting on the edge of the floor, down over the crack between the floor and the plasterboard. I cut a few lengths and brush them with oil with added white pigment, so they will be ready when the wall of the stairway is finished.

The first wall we reach is that of the existing stairwell. While Dan continues laying the rest of the floor toward the bathroom wall, I erect a wall for the bedroom on the already laid boards. For a moment we can enjoy the sight of the floor in its full length before I spoil it by building the wall. Jens and Fredrik will now get their bedroom.

A newly laid floor is wonderful. Dan's line dance was appropriate on the chipboard subfloor, but a polonaise would be more apt here. He is not up for it, however, even though they are playing Roky Erickson on the radio and it does not get any better than that.

"It turned out well; we were lucky this time," I say.

All floors face damage through use, get scratches and dents, and a pine floor, being soft, is particularly vulnerable. I usually suggest to customers that I can put it through a little wear and tear before delivery for an additional fee. They can then relax that little bit more when moving in, as they do not need to worry about the floor so much. Once the floor has seen a little use, their lives will be more relaxed; the children can play freely without the parents getting stressed out every time they hear something hitting the floor with a bang.

Even though I have yet to have someone take me up on my offer, it is a way to get the customer to stop and think while they laugh at my absurd proposal. That brief moment before they realize I am joking is fun.

In any case, we are always thorough and cautious when we lay a floor, and carry it out as painstakingly as making a piece of furniture, free of error, with no dents or nicks.

47

THE WALL IS FINISHED; THE PAINTERS JUST NEED TO do the skim work and painting, and are already hard at it. They will soon have it done. The Petersens opted for the slightly more expensive, hard-wearing paint and that will stand them in good stead over time. Dan has finished laying the floor and is now busy with the bedroom door, as well as all the casings and all manner of odds and ends. We put on the pre-painted skirting boards, and then the painters use Polyfilla to fill in the holes left by nails and to skim any cracks, before giving everything a final coat.

The opening for the new stairs is my job.

I remove the chipboard from over the hole and all the material now to be taken out: insulation, the redundant floor joists, and the 1.5 by 3.75-inch plank we used when laying the subfloor. Now only the ceiling below divides the loft from the apartment. For safety I place two 2×4s across the hole. With Dan's help, we replace the chipboard we had removed partially over the hole so it is possible to work between the two floors. To prevent dust from below coming up, on top of the chipboard I lay plastic sheeting that extends a little over our newly laid floor. Now the loft is the new space and needs to be protected.

Our completion date is three weeks away, but we only have

a week of work left. I had a realistic deadline in the agreement and we have maintained steady progress throughout the project. But we seldom have so much time at the end of a job.

You do not go empty-handed when there is something to be carried, so before leaving for the weekend we take what we can down to my van. The job is beginning to wind down.

On Monday morning the family are running a little late and Jens and Fredrik are racing around when I come down into the apartment with my tools and materials to get set up to work on the new opening. The boys have heard that the hole in the roof is being made today and the staircase is coming. They are excited, and with good cause; it is a special day, as the apartment and loft are to be properly joined into one.

Jens decides he wants to stay home to watch us make the hole in the ceiling. He has a minor tantrum when he is not allowed to, only calming down when Dan uses a bit of his customer service charms.

He explains that we cover up around where we work, so there will not be much to see, and anyway it is dangerous for children to be around when demolition is being carried out. Carpentry is exciting, but it can be noisy and scary too, he tells him. Jens says he understands.

"You can both see it when you get home from school later. There'll be a big hole there then," Dan says, pointing up.

"And that's where the staircase is going," Fredrik says.

They wonder where the staircase is, if I have it in the van. I explain that it is coming later, in a while, that other people are bringing it. But they will get to see the hole today.

In order to save time I carried out some preparatory work before the weekend. I cut laths, found what was needed to seal off the area around the hole for the staircase, and left it lying ready in the loft. Dan helps me out; it is easier when we are two. We place drywall sheets on the floor of the apartment beneath and using plastic sheeting for walls, make a room to work in. The sheeting is kept taut by a framework of laths. We tape it to the ceiling and walls to close the space off completely. All we lack is a door, and with one cut of a knife we have a slit that can be taped up again when I enter the space to start the demolition work. This is a dust-proof construction and dust cannot enter the loft above either, so demolition work can begin.

Plaster ceilings are fragile and the problem with tearing them out is that they can easily come apart. A saw can handle wood, an angle grinder with a diamond-cutting disc can tackle plaster, but I do not have a tool that can handle both materials when I need to cut cleanly. The solution is to take one thing at a time.

Using my small angle grinder, and hooking it up to my vacuum attachment, I cut into the plaster right through to the boards they are fixed to, hardly causing any dust. Now I can tear out the plaster in the ceiling where the opening for the stairs is to go. I then pick up the reciprocating saw and cut the boards, letting everything fall onto the drywall sheets protecting the floor of the apartment below. We have our hole, without any damage to the rest of the ceiling.

I tidy and vacuum thoroughly inside our dust tent. Then I attach drywall to the sides of the stairwell just under the floor we laid in the loft, before putting corner bead, angled metal strips, in place. They give a solid external angle at the intersecting surfaces that the painter can plaster along. The ceiling is in good condition and will not need any skim besides what is to be done around the hole. Tam is working up in the loft and comes down to apply a first coat.

Three of the sides will be covered by drywall, while

the mason will render the fourth. Johannes drops by in the afternoon and applies the first layer of mortar on the part of the wall that the floor used to cover.

Our construction site is now in the heart of the apartment. Although there is not much work to be done, it must feel like a veritable invasion to the Petersens. To improve matters for them we take down our plastic sheeting and remove the plasterboards from the floor. The painter takes extra care with the skimming to avoid any mess. He needs to sand a little after the final layer though, so he tapes some plastic sheeting to the roof that stretches to the floor to avoid any dust getting into the apartment.

All the filling and skimming has been done in the loft so we vacuum it completely and go over it with a dry microfiber mop afterward. There is some Ikea furniture to go in the living-room area of the loft but it only needs to be assembled, not customized, and that will only take a couple of hours.

The very last piece of carpentry required of us is to loosely secure the casing to the floorboards in the new stairwell. The man who puts in the staircase can remove these and fit them back into place afterward. The Petersens' staircase is arriving soon and they only need to wait a little longer before they can put the loft to use. I find it appropriate that the casing that marks the transition from apartment to loft should bring our carpentry work here to a conclusion.

The painter is finishing up, allowing the electrician the opportunity to mount all his boxes, put in lights and switches, and then all the electrics will be done.

So it is Tam and Bjørn Olav who put the finishing touches on the work. It looks nice when the last of the skirting boards is painted and the lights can be put on.

It is a bit of an anticlimax, really. So much work, such big changes, so much time, all ebbing out in small chores, tidying up, and lugging tools down to the van. Our lunch today is the last time we will eat in the Petersens' kitchen. We drink coffee afterward and raise a cup for a successful project.

I take a long weekend and do some paperwork in between fishing and sleeping.

The photographs of the entire job need to be sorted and put into my system, papers need to be tidied, and the budget for the project needs to be compared to the financial return.

Money? My quote was almost bang on.

My budget for the subcontractors' work tallied with their costs. Dan delivered time sheets and was paid as we went along and I have taken out wages as required. I have written out my own time sheet and kept a running record of hours spent and material costs on a spreadsheet. Whatever is left over after all the expenses have been put in are my earnings. I can afford a summer holiday and have a healthy buffer in my bank account when autumn comes.

Money matters, of course, and has played a role in this story, but as always it matters less when it does not represent a problem, and that is why it has not been mentioned along the way.

This has been my project, but on the next job Dan will be the boss and I will not have the final responsibility. I will work, fill in time sheets, and hand invoices over to him. I will not need to attend meetings in the planning phase, prepare documentation, or think too much about budgets or finances. That will be like having time off too; just working, letting Dan bear the administrative load.

48

EARLY SUMMER, AND THE DAYS ARE GETTING WARMER
as we hold our completion meeting. There is a big difference
between the first time I saw the site in the November darkness
and now, in this light green time of year. Kari's father looks
after the boys while Kari, Jon, and I go through the work that
has been carried out. Dan, Tam, Bjørn Olav, Thomas, Johannes,
Gustav, Jukka, Petter, and I have all left a little part of ourselves
in these walls and ceilings now.

We move around the loft. In our hands we hold copies of
the specifications and the list of work to be done that accompa-
nied the contract we signed. We check the work, item by item,
and tick it off as being completed and approved by the client. It
does not take long and although mostly a formality, it is
important. We have shown them the work we have done along
the way and discussed solutions but in the end Kari and Jon
made the final choices. In that sense, they have been in control
and I am confident that they will be satisfied.

They assume responsibility for the loft now and I can let go.
Once they have given the floor a look-over and signed off on it
as being laid satisfactorily, then any scratches on it are theirs,
and no longer anything I need to worry about.

The signatures we now sign feel like the last word in a

story. A story that began with the same words: the signatures on the contract we signed at the start of January.

It seems like ages ago since we spoke for the first time and a long time since the space we are now standing in was bare, so we reminisce as we go along. When we get to the bathroom, Kari says she is glad they went for the handmade oak furniture. Looking at how it turned out she thinks it almost odd they were even considering Ikea. When we look up at the roof to certify they are happy with all the work carried out there, we see the support beam running the length of it and are reminded of the struts and ties at floor level that were removed.

Kari and Jon are happy with the solid wood floor and think it was nicely laid. They say that friends who have been to visit have been particularly impressed with the aspen paneling in the bathroom. They tell me that Fredrik and Jens talk about everything they have seen in the loft, about the drawings they made and the boat that they have now sailed at the cottage. They think the boys are going to miss us. They say what the papers cannot, that they are glad we came and converted their loft. Their voices have a happy tone. I too am happy.

We have been so prominent in their daily life, with our noise and dust, with the invoices I have written, with greeting one another every Monday morning, that the Petersens are no doubt happy it is all behind them. That is how it is, and it is understandable. No matter how satisfied you are with your tradesmen it is good to stop seeing them every day.

Dan's clients are waiting for us at their house in Grefsen. We are going to replace all the windows, remove the exterior siding and put in additional insulation before putting new paneling up. A pleasant job now that summer has come and the days are warmer. We have holidays coming before we finish that job, then there is a kitchen to install in Gamlebyen.

No one knows what the future holds or where our vans will be headed after that.

GLOSSARY

ANGLE GRINDER A handheld power tool fitted with a cutting or grinding disc that runs parallel to the body of the tool. Widely used in metalworking and construction.

ASPEN A fairly soft white wood containing very little resin, which weathers well and has low flammability. It is ideal for use in saunas, as it does not get too warm, and for bathrooms as it handles humidity particularly well. It is not often used for flooring due to its softness.

BATTENS Thin, narrow strips of wood used to seal, reinforce, or support a joint or panel.

BIRD'S BEAK CUT (or birdsmouth joint) An indentation cut into a rafter consisting of a "seat cut" (the face of which rests on the top plate) and a "heel cut" or "plumb cut" (the face of which lies parallel to the supporting wall), forming a shape that resembles a bird's mouth.

BULLDOG-TOOTHED PLATE CONNECTORS Single- and double-sided toothed plate connectors used for improving bolt performance in timber by increasing joist strength.

CARPENTER/CARPENTRY In the context of an ongoing construction job, carpenters usually work on-site. Their specialized skill is in dealing with wooden fixtures, such as fitting floors and staircases, window frames, cupboards, and shelving.

CHALK LINE A tool for marking long, straight lines on relatively flat surfaces, by the action of a taut nylon or other string with a hook or loop at the free end, coated with a loose dye, usually chalk.

CHERRY PICKER A hydraulic crane with a secured platform at the end of its telescopic or articulated arm, used for raising and lowering workers.

CHICKEN RAMP An inclined plank with transverse cleats.

COLLAR BEAMS A horizontal piece of squared timber connecting two rafters and thereby forming an A-shaped roof structure.

DRYWALL A board made of plaster set between two sheets of heavy-duty paper, used especially to form or line the inner walls of houses.

DRYWALL LIFT An articulated device to facilitate the handling and lifting of drywall panels to ceiling height for easy fixing.

FLASHING Strips of nonferrous metal, folded to cover the joint between the wall and the roof at the gable ends of buildings, to make it waterproof. Also used around chimneys and roof vent covers.

FORCED-ACTION MIXER An easy-to-transport, motorized mixer that uses a rotating drum or rotating paddles. Components such as sand and cement are turned and folded by a fast and efficient action into a homogeneous mixture.

GROOVE PLANKS Planks with a groove designed to capture planks with a tongue. This assembly is known as "tongue and groove." A groove plank may also be used to lock a thinner piece in place, for example in cabinetmaking.

GYPSUM A building plaster that may be used on a wide variety of background types, including concrete, brick, metal lath, and drywall.

HOUSING COOPERATIVE A type of housing, common in Norway, in which residents form a corporation for the purpose of owning and managing a property collectively. Residents own shares in the corporation, which gives them the right to live in a specific apartment rather than own individual units. Rent is paid proportional to the size of the apartments. Cooperatives are governed by majority decisions by shareholders.

JOINER/JOINERY The specialization of the joiner in construction work is in making the components, such as windows and window frames, doors and doorframes, trusses, staircases, etc.

JOIST A length of timber or steel supporting part of the structure of a building, typically arranged in parallel series to support a floor or ceiling.

KNEE WALL A low wall, typically under 40 inches in height, used to support the rafters in timber roof construction.

LATH Commonly a smaller, thin strip of wood (e.g., 5/16 × 1.5 inches) with a variety of functions, for example as battens for roof slates, or as nailing strips.

MASON/MASONRY A mason builds structures from individual components such as brick, stone, or tiles, bound together by mortar. They also commonly work with concrete.

MASTER CARPENTER After working as an apprentice and then as a journeyman, a carpenter may go on to study or test as a master carpenter. In some countries this is a rigorous and expensive process, requiring extensive knowledge (including economic and legal knowledge) and skill to achieve master certification. Some countries generally require master status for anyone employing and teaching apprentices in the craft. In Norway it is a fairly extensive formal education, and a formally protected title.

MITER JOINT A joint made by beveling each of two parts to be joined at a certain angle. For instance to form a corner, a 90-degree angle.

MITER SAW (also known as a drop saw) A handsaw used with a miter box or a circular saw on a swiveling base or table designed to make clean and accurate angle cuts.

MUSIC Research carried out by this carpenter proves that these albums are good to work to: *Safe as Milk* by Captain Beefheart, *The Evil One* by Roky Erickson, and *Mission to Mir* by the Beat Tornados.

NAILING STRIPS, see also STEEL STRIP and LATH Any strip of material attached to a hard surface, onto which another material such as a timber frame, beam, drywall, etc., may be nailed (or more commonly screwed). Steel strips perforated down the center may have the same function.

NRK The Norwegian national broadcasting company.

A PASSIVE HOUSE A rigorous, voluntary standard for energy efficiency in a building to reduce its ecological footprint. It results in ultralow-energy buildings that require little energy for heating or cooling. The standard varies from country to country, and there are plans to make it compulsory in Norway.

PLUMB BOB (or plummet) A weight, usually with a pointed tip on the bottom, suspended from a string and used as a vertical reference line, or "plumb line." Essentially the vertical equivalent of a water level.

PLUNGE SAW A power-driven circular saw that can "plunge" or cut down into the material to make straight cuts when used in conjunction with a "track" or "guide." The plunge is possible due to the absence of a fixed riving knife (safety device).

PURLIN A longitudinal piece in a roof frame.

RAFTER A beam forming part of the internal framework of a roof.

RECIPROCATING SAW Also known as a "saber" saw, cuts through a push-and-pull ("reciprocating") motion of the blade.

RELATIVE HUMIDITY The measurement of the amount of water vapor present in air expressed as a percentage of the amount needed for saturation at the same temperature. Warm air will "hold" more moisture than cold air before condensation occurs.

ROOF TRUSS A timber roof truss is a structural framework of timbers designed to bridge the space above a room and to provide support for a roof. Trusses usually occur at regular intervals, linked by longitudinal timbers such as purlins.

SCRIBING Using a handheld pointed tool, not unlike a compass, to mark or score metal or wood to be cut. Scribes are mostly used to mark materials where they are being fitted to an uneven or irregular surface.

SNAP-OFF KNIFE A retractable utility knife. A segment of the long blade can be snapped off to the next segment when blunt.

SOCIAL DUMPING The practice of some employers of lowering wages and cutting employees' benefits for competitive advantage and in order to increase profit margins. Migrant workers, often attracted by false promises, are especially vulnerable to this practice.

SOIL PIPES Pipes for removal of wastewater and sewage to the outside of a building, necessarily ventilated at the top.

STANLEY KNIFE A workplace utility knife with a fixed blade, used for general or utility purposes, commonly referred to by its trademark.

STEEL STRIP, see also **NAILING STRIPS** Flexible, bendable metal used as nailing strips for drywall, for example. It often comes on a roll, is perforated down the center, and may be used to stabilize corners, especially when joining two components.

STRING Fixed taut between two points in order to achieve a straight line, string is one of the carpenter's most useful tools. In fact, it is also indispensable in masonry work and many other crafts.

STRUT A structural component used to support, and therefore designed to withstand longitudinal compression.

SUBFLOOR A base flooring layer onto which flooring material or a finished floor may be laid.

TIE A structural component or beam used for tension rather than compression (see STRUT) between rafters.

TONGUE PLANKS Used in conjunction with groove planks, they form a mortise-and-tenon joint along their lengths.

TORPEDO LEVEL A type of spirit level with three spirit tubes for measuring horizontal, vertical, and diagonal planes.

TRIMMER A timber beam used in framing construction to create an opening around a stairwell, for instance. Trimmers are installed parallel to the primary floor joists and support the headers running perpendicular to the primary joists.

TRY SQUARE A tool used for marking and measuring a piece of wood. The square refers to the tool's primary use of measuring the accuracy of a right angle; to "try" a surface is to check its straightness or correspondence to an adjoining surface.

WINDPROOF SHEATHING Acts as a membrane to protect against wind, dust, and weather.

WOOD PLUGGING A technique used to conceal screwheads in simple joinery. Countersunk holes are "plugged" with wooden plugs cut from the same timber and glued into position.